Langston Hug

VINTAGE **HUG**

Langston Hughes was born in Joplin, Missouri, in 1902. By the time he enrolled in Columbia University he had already launched his literary career with his poem "The Negro Speaks of Rivers," published in *Crisis* in 1921. Often regarded as "the poet laureate of Harlem," Hughes was a central figure in the Harlem Renaissance of the 1920s. Known for his insightful, colorful portrayals of black life in America from the 1920s to the 1960s, Hughes published more than thirty-five books of poetry, fiction, short stories, children's poetry, musicals, operas, autobiography, scripts, and essays.

Throughout his life Hughes was a devoted fan of black music, and he fused together jazz and blues with traditional verse in his first two books, *The Weary Blues* and *Fine Clothes to the Jew.* He was also well known for his creation of the fictional character Jesse B. Semple, nicknamed Simple, who satirized racial injustices. In 1929, Hughes earned his B.A. from Lincoln University in Pennsylvania, where he was later presented with an honorary Litt.D. Over the course of his life, Hughes was also awarded a Guggenheim Fellowship (1935), a Rosenwald Fellowship (1940), and an American Academy of Arts and Letters Grant (1947). Hughes died in 1967. Through his work condemning racism and celebrating African-American culture, Langston Hughes became one of the most influential and esteemed writers of the twentieth century.

Poetry

The Weary Blues
Fine Clothes to the Jew
The Dream-Keeper
Shakespeare in Harlem
Fields of Wonder
One-Way Ticket
Montage of a Dream Deferred
Selected Poems of Langston Hughes
Ask Your Mama
The Panther and the Lash

Fiction

Not Without Laughter
Laughing to Keep from Crying
The Sweet Flypaper of Life
Something in Common and Other Stories
Five Plays by Langston Hughes

Humor

Simple Speaks His Mind
Simple Takes a Wife
Simple Stakes a Claim
Best of Simple
Simple's Uncle Sam

For Young People

The First Book of the Negroes
The First Book of Jazz
The First Book of Rhythms
The First Book of the West Indies
The First Book of Africa

—with Arna Bontemps
Popo and Fifina

Biography and Autobiography

The Big Sea
Famous American Negroes
Famous Negro Music-Makers
I Wonder As I Wander
Famous Negro Heroes of America

Anthology

The Langston Hughes Reader

History

Fight for Freedom: The Story of the NAACP

—with Milton Meltzer
A Pictorial History of the Negro in America
Black Magic: A Pictorial History of the Negro
in American Entertainment

VINTAGE HUGHES

Langston Hughes

VINTAGE BOOKS

A Division of Random House, Inc.

New York

A VINTAGE ORIGINAL, JANUARY 2004

Copyright © 2004 by the Estate of Langston Hughes

All rights reserved under International and Pan-American
Copyright Conventions. Published in the United States by
Vintage Books, a division of Random House, Inc., New York,
and simultaneously in Canada by Random House
of Canada Limited, Toronto.

Vintage and colophon are registered trademarks
of Random House, Inc.

"Cora Unashamed," "Home," and "The Blues I'm Playing" are from
The Ways of White Folks, copyright © 1933, 1934 by Alfred A. Knopf, Inc.,
copyright renewed 1962 by Langston Hughes (Vintage Books, 1990).
All the other selections included in this anthology are from
The Collected Poems of Langston Hughes, copyright © 1994
by the Estate of Langston Hughes (Vintage Books, 1995).

Library of Congress Cataloging-in-Publication Data
Hughes, Langston, 1902–1967.
Vintage Hughes / Langston Hughes.
p.   cm.
ISBN 1-4000-3402-7
1. African Americans—Literary collections.
I. Title.
PS3515.U274 A6   2004
811'.52—dc22   2003060816

Book design by JoAnne Metsch

www.vintagebooks.com

Printed in the United States of America
10   9   8   7   6   5   4   3   2   1

CONTENTS

From *The Collected Poems of Langston Hughes*

From *The Ways of White Folks*

VINTAGE HUGHES

The Negro Speaks of Rivers

I've known rivers:
I've known rivers ancient as the world and older than the
　　flow of human blood in human veins.

My soul has grown deep like the rivers.

I bathed in the Euphrates when dawns were young.
I built my hut near the Congo and it lulled me to sleep.
I looked upon the Nile and raised the pyramids above it.
I heard the singing of the Mississippi when Abe Lincoln
　　went down to New Orleans, and I've seen its muddy
　　bosom turn all golden in the sunset.

I've known rivers:
Ancient, dusky rivers.

My soul has grown deep like the rivers.

Aunt Sue's Stories

Aunt Sue has a head full of stories.
Aunt Sue has a whole heart full of stories.
Summer nights on the front porch
Aunt Sue cuddles a brown-faced child to her bosom
And tells him stories.

Black slaves
Working in the hot sun,
And black slaves
Walking in the dewy night,
And black slaves
Singing sorrow songs on the banks of a mighty river
Mingle themselves softly
In the flow of old Aunt Sue's voice,
Mingle themselves softly
In the dark shadows that cross and recross
Aunt Sue's stories.

And the dark-faced child, listening,
Knows that Aunt Sue's stories are real stories.
He knows that Aunt Sue never got her stories
Out of any book at all,
But that they came
Right out of her own life.

The dark-faced child is quiet
Of a summer night
Listening to Aunt Sue's stories.

Negro

I am a Negro:
>   Black as the night is black,
>   Black like the depths of my Africa.

I've been a slave:
>   Caesar told me to keep his door-steps clean.
>   I brushed the boots of Washington.

I've been a worker:
>   Under my hands the pyramids arose.
>   I made mortar for the Woolworth Building.

I've been a singer:
>   All the way from Africa to Georgia
>   I carried my sorrow songs.
>   I made ragtime.

I've been a victim:
>   The Belgians cut off my hands in the Congo.
>   They lynch me still in Mississippi.

I am a Negro:
>   Black as the night is black,
>   Black like the depths of my Africa.

Mexican Market Woman

This ancient hag
Who sits upon the ground
Selling her scanty wares
Day in, day round,
Has known high wind-swept mountains,
And the sun has made
Her skin so brown.

The South

The lazy, laughing South
With blood on its mouth.
The sunny-faced South,
     Beast-strong,
     Idiot-brained.
The child-minded South
Scratching in the dead fire's ashes
For a Negro's bones.
     Cotton and the moon,
     Warmth, earth, warmth,
     The sky, the sun, the stars,
     The magnolia-scented South.
Beautiful, like a woman,

Seductive as a dark-eyed whore,
        Passionate, cruel,
        Honey-lipped, syphilitic—
        That is the South.
And I, who am black, would love her
But she spits in my face.
And I, who am black,
Would give her many rare gifts
But she turns her back upon me.
        So now I seek the North—
        The cold-faced North,
        For she, they say,
        Is a kinder mistress,
And in her house my children
May escape the spell of the South.

Mother to Son

Well, son, I'll tell you:
Life for me ain't been no crystal stair.
It's had tacks in it,
And splinters,
And boards torn up,
And places with no carpet on the floor—
Bare.
But all the time

I'se been a-climbin' on,
And reachin' landin's,
And turnin' corners,
And sometimes goin' in the dark
Where there ain't been no light.
So boy, don't you turn back.
Don't you set down on the steps
'Cause you finds it's kinder hard.
Don't you fall now—
For I'se still goin', honey,
I'se still climbin',
And life for me ain't been no crystal stair.

When Sue Wears Red

When Susanna Jones wears red
Her face is like an ancient cameo
Turned brown by the ages.

Come with a blast of trumpets,
        Jesus!

When Susanna Jones wears red
A queen from some time-dead Egyptian night
Walks once again.

Blow trumpets,
        Jesus!

And the beauty of Susanna Jones in red
Burns in my heart a love-fire sharp like pain.

Sweet silver trumpets,
        Jesus!

A Black Pierrot

I am a black Pierrot:
        She did not love me,
        So I crept away into the night
        And the night was black, too.

I am a black Pierrot:
        She did not love me,
        So I wept until the dawn
        Dripped blood over the eastern hills
        And my heart was bleeding, too.

I am a black Pierrot:
        She did not love me,
        So with my once gay-colored soul
        Shrunken like a balloon without air,
        I went forth in the morning
        To seek a new brown love.

My People

The night is beautiful,
So the faces of my people.

The stars are beautiful,
So the eyes of my people.

Beautiful, also, is the sun.
Beautiful, also, are the souls of my people.

Dream Variations

To fling my arms wide
In some place of the sun,
To whirl and to dance
Till the white day is done.
Then rest at cool evening
Beneath a tall tree
While night comes on gently,
        Dark like me—
That is my dream!

To fling my arms wide
In the face of the sun,
Dance! Whirl! Whirl!
Till the quick day is done.

Rest at pale evening . . .
A tall, slim tree . . .
Night coming tenderly
    Black like me.

Troubled Woman

She stands
In the quiet darkness,
This troubled woman
Bowed by
Weariness and pain
Like an
Autumn flower
In the frozen rain,
Like a
Wind-blown autumn flower
That never lifts its head
Again.

I, Too

I, too, sing America.

I am the darker brother.
They send me to eat in the kitchen
When company comes,
But I laugh,
And eat well,
And grow strong.

Tomorrow,
I'll be at the table
When company comes.
Nobody'll dare
Say to me,
"Eat in the kitchen,"
Then.

Besides,
They'll see how beautiful I am
And be ashamed—

I, too, am America.

The Weary Blues

Droning a drowsy syncopated tune,
Rocking back and forth to a mellow croon,
    I heard a Negro play.
Down on Lenox Avenue the other night
By the pale dull pallor of an old gas light
    He did a lazy sway. . . .
    He did a lazy sway. . . .
To the tune o' those Weary Blues.
With his ebony hands on each ivory key
He made that poor piano moan with melody.
    O Blues!
Swaying to and fro on his rickety stool
He played that sad raggy tune like a musical fool.
    Sweet Blues!
Coming from a black man's soul.
    O Blues!
In a deep song voice with a melancholy tone
I heard that Negro sing, that old piano moan—
    "Ain't got nobody in all this world,
        Ain't got nobody but ma self.
        I's gwine to quit ma frownin'
        And put ma troubles on the shelf."

Thump, thump, thump, went his foot on the floor.
He played a few chords then he sang some more—
    "I got the Weary Blues
        And I can't be satisfied.
        Got the Weary Blues

And can't be satisfied—
I ain't happy no mo'
And I wish that I had died."
And far into the night he crooned that tune.
The stars went out and so did the moon.
The singer stopped playing and went to bed
While the Weary Blues echoed through his head.
He slept like a rock or a man that's dead.

America

Little dark baby,
Little Jew baby,
Little outcast,
America is seeking the stars,
America is seeking tomorrow.
You are America.
I am America
America—the dream,
America—the vision.
America—the star-seeking I.
Out of yesterday
The chains of slavery;
Out of yesterday,
The ghettos of Europe;
Out of yesterday,
The poverty and pain of the old, old world,
The building and struggle of this new one,

We come
You and I,
Seeking the stars.
You and I,
You of the blue eyes
And the blond hair,
I of the dark eyes
And the crinkly hair.
You and I
Offering hands
Being brothers,
Being one,
Being America.
You and I.
And I?
Who am I?
You know me:
I am Crispus Attucks at the Boston Tea Party;
Jimmy Jones in the ranks of the last black troops
    marching for democracy.
I am Sojourner Truth preaching and praying
    for the goodness of this wide, wide land;
Today's black mother bearing tomorrow's America.
Who am I?
You know me,
Dream of my dreams,
I am America.
I am America seeking the stars.
America—
Hoping, praying
Fighting, dreaming.

Knowing
There are stains
On the beauty of my democracy,
I want to be clean.
I want to grovel
No longer in the mire.
I want to reach always
After stars.
Who am I?
I am the ghetto child,
I am the dark baby,
I am you
And the blond tomorrow
And yet
I am my one sole self,
America seeking the stars.

Cross

My old man's a white old man
And my old mother's black.
If ever I cursed my white old man
I take my curses back.

If ever I cursed my black old mother
And wished she were in hell,

I'm sorry for that evil wish
And now I wish her well.

My old man died in a fine big house.
My ma died in a shack.
I wonder where I'm gonna die,
Being neither white nor black?

Young Sailor

He carries
His own strength
And his own laughter,
His own today
And his own hereafter—
This strong young sailor
Of the wide seas.

What is money for?
To spend, he says.
And wine?
To drink.
And women?
To love.
And today?
For joy.

And the green sea
For strength,
And the brown land
For laughter.

And nothing hereafter.

Joy

I went to look for Joy,
Slim, dancing Joy,
Gay, laughing Joy,
Bright-eyed Joy—
And I found her
Driving the butcher's cart
In the arms of the butcher boy!
Such company, such company,
As keeps this young nymph, Joy!

Ruby Brown

She was young and beautiful
And golden like the sunshine
That warmed her body.
And because she was colored

Mayville had no place to offer her,
Nor fuel for the clean flame of joy
That tried to burn within her soul.

One day,
Sitting on old Mrs. Latham's back porch
Polishing the silver,
She asked herself two questions
And they ran something like this:
What can a colored girl do
On the money from a white woman's kitchen?
And ain't there any joy in this town?

Now the streets down by the river
Know more about this pretty Ruby Brown,
And the sinister shuttered houses of the bottoms
Hold a yellow girl
Seeking an answer to her questions.
The good church folk do not mention
Her name any more.

But the white men,
Habitués of the high shuttered houses,
Pay more money to her now
Than they ever did before,
When she worked in their kitchens.

Back Luck Card

Cause you don't love me
Is awful, awful hard.
Gypsy done showed me
My bad luck card.

There ain't no good left
In this world for me.
Gypsy done tole me—
Unlucky as can be.

I don't know what
Po' weary me can do.
Gypsy says I'd kill my self
If I was you.

Feet o' Jesus

At the feet o' Jesus,
Sorrow like a sea.
Lordy, let yo' mercy
Come driftin' down on me.

At the feet o' Jesus
At yo' feet I stand.
O, ma little Jesus,
Please reach out yo' hand.

A House in Taos

Rain

Thunder of the Rain God:
    And we three
    Smitten by beauty.

Thunder of the Rain God:
    And we three
    Weary, weary.

Thunder of the Rain God:
    And you, she, and I
    Waiting for nothingness.

Do you understand the stillness
    Of this house
    In Taos
Under the thunder of the Rain God?

Sun

That there should be a barren garden
About this house in Taos
Is not so strange,
But that there should be three barren hearts
In this one house in Taos—
Who carries ugly things to show the sun?

Moon

Did you ask for the beaten brass of the moon?
We can buy lovely things with money,
You, she, and I,
Yet you seek,
As though you could keep,
This unbought loveliness of moon.

Wind

Touch our bodies, wind.
Our bodies are separate, individual things.
Touch our bodies, wind,
But blow quickly
Through the red, white, yellow skins
Of our bodies
To the terrible snarl,
Not mine,
Not yours,
Not hers,
But all one snarl of souls.
Blow quickly, wind,
Before we run back
Into the windlessness—
With our bodies—
Into the windlessness
Of our house in Taos.

Brass Spittoons

Clean the spittoons, boy.
   Detroit,
   Chicago,
   Atlantic City,
   Palm Beach.
Clean the spittoons.
The steam in hotel kitchens,
And the smoke in hotel lobbies,
And the slime in hotel spittoons:
Part of my life.
   Hey, boy!
   A nickel,
   A dime,
   A dollar,
Two dollars a day.
   Hey, boy!
   A nickel,
   A dime,
   A dollar,
   Two dollars
Buys shoes for the baby.
House rent to pay.
Gin on Saturday,
Church on Sunday.
   My God!
Babies and gin and church
and women and Sunday
all mixed up with dimes and

dollars and clean spittoons
and house rent to pay.
    Hey, boy!
A bright bowl of brass is beautiful to the Lord.
Bright polished brass like the cymbals
Of King David's dancers,
Like the wine cups of Solomon.
    Hey, boy!
A clean spittoon on the altar of the Lord.
A clean bright spittoon all newly polished,—
At least I can offer that.
    Come 'ere, boy!

Midnight Dancer

(To a Black Dancer in "The Little Savoy")

Wine-maiden
Of the jazz-tuned night,
Lips
Sweet as purple dew,
Breasts
Like the pillows of all sweet dreams,
Who crushed
The grapes of joy
And dripped their juice
On you?

Harlem Night Song

Come,
Let us roam the night together
Singing.

I love you.

Across
The Harlem roof-tops
Moon is shining.
Night sky is blue.
Stars are great drops
Of golden dew.

Down the street
A band is playing.

I love you.

Come,
Let us roam the night together
Singing.

Ardella

I would liken you
To a night without stars
Were it not for your eyes.
I would liken you
To a sleep without dreams
Were it not for your songs.

Port Town

Hello, sailor boy,
In from the sea!
Hello, sailor,
Come with me!

Come on drink cognac.
Rather have wine?
Come here, I love you.
Come and be mine.

Lights, sailor boy,
Warm, white lights.
Solid land, kid.
Wild, white nights.

Come on, sailor,
Out o' the sea.
Let's go, sweetie!
Come with me.

Death of an Old Seaman

We buried him high on a windy hill,
But his soul went out to sea.
I know, for I heard, when all was still,
His sea-soul say to me:

Put no tombstone at my head,
For here I do not make my bed.
Strew no flowers on my grave,
I've gone back to the wind and wave.
Do not, do not weep for me,
For I am happy with my sea.

Fire

Fire,
Fire, Lord!
Fire gonna burn ma soul!

I ain't been good,
I ain't been clean—
I been stinkin', low-down, mean.

Fire,
Fire, Lord!
Fire gonna burn ma soul!

Tell me, brother,
Do you believe
If you wanta go to heaben
Got to moan an' grieve?

Fire,
Fire, Lord!
Fire gonna burn ma soul!

I been stealin',
Been tellin' lies,
Had more women
Than Pharaoh had wives.

Fire,
Fire, Lord!
Fire gonna burn ma soul!
I means Fire, Lord!
Fire gonna burn ma soul!

Lover's Return

My old time daddy
Came back home last night.
His face was pale and
His eyes didn't look just right.

He says, "Mary, I'm
Comin' home to you—
So sick and lonesome
I don't know what to do."

Oh, men treats women
Just like a pair o' shoes—
You kicks 'em round and
Does 'em like you choose.

I looked at my daddy—
Lawd! and I wanted to cry.
He looked so thin—
Lawd! that I wanted to cry.
But the devil told me:
Damn a lover
Come home to die!

Afro-American Fragment

So long,
So far away
Is Africa.
Not even memories alive
Save those that history books create,
Save those that songs
Beat back into the blood—
Beat out of blood with words sad-sung
In strange un-Negro tongue—
So long,
So far away
Is Africa.

Subdued and time-lost
Are the drums—and yet
Through some vast mist of race
There comes this song
I do not understand
This song of atavistic land,
Of bitter yearnings lost
Without a place—
So long,
So far away
Is Africa's
Dark face.

Drum

Bear in mind
That death is a drum
Beating forever
Till the last worms come
To answer its call,
Till the last stars fall,
Until the last atom
Is no atom at all,
Until time is lost
And there is no air
And space itself
Is nothing nowhere,
Death is a drum,
A signal drum,
Calling life
To come!
Come!
Come!

Sylvester's Dying Bed

I woke up this mornin'
'Bout half-past three.
All the womens in town
Was gathered round me.

Sweet gals was a–moanin',
"Sylvester's gonna die!"
And a hundred pretty mamas
Bowed their heads to cry.

I woke up little later
'Bout half-past fo',
The doctor 'n' undertaker's
Both at ma do'.

Black gals was a-beggin',
"You can't leave us here!"
Brown-skins cryin', "Daddy!
Honey! Baby! Don't go, dear!"

But I felt ma time's a-comin',
And I know'd I's dyin' fast
I seed the River Jerden
A-creepin' muddy past—
But I's still Sweet Papa 'Vester,
Yes, sir! Long as life do last!

So I hollers, "Com'ere, babies,
Fo' to love yo' daddy right!"
And I reaches up to hug 'em—
When the Lawd put out the light.

Then everything was darkness
In a great . . . big . . . night.

October 16: The Raid

Perhaps
You will remember
John Brown.

John Brown
Who took his gun,
Took twenty-one companions
White and black,
Went to shoot your way to freedom
Where two rivers meet
And the hills of the
North
And the hills of the
South
Look slow at one another—
And died
For your sake.

Now that you are
Many years free,
And the echo of the Civil War
Has passed away,
And Brown himself
Has long been tried at law,
Hanged by the neck,
And buried in the ground—
Since Harpers Ferry
Is alive with ghosts today,

Immortal raiders
Come again to town—

Perhaps
You will recall
John Brown.

Scottsboro

8 BLACK BOYS IN A SOUTHERN JAIL.
   WORLD, TURN PALE!

8 black boys and one white lie.
Is it much to die?

Is it much to die when immortal feet
March with you down Time's street,
When beyond steel bars sound the deathless drums
Like a mighty heart-beat as They come?

Who comes?

Christ,
Who fought alone.

John Brown.

That mad mob
That tore the Bastille down
Stone by stone.

Moses.

Jeanne d'Arc.

Dessalines.

Nat Turner.

Fighters for the free.

Lenin with the flag blood red.

(Not dead! Not dead!
None of those is dead.)

Gandhi.

Sandino.

Evangelista, too,
To walk with you—

8 Black Boys in a Southern Jail.
World, Turn Pale!

The Negro Mother

Children, I come back today
To tell you a story of the long dark way
That I had to climb, that I had to know
In order that the race might live and grow.
Look at my face—dark as the night—
Yet shining like the sun with love's true light.
I am the child they stole from the sand
Three hundred years ago in Africa's land.
I am the dark girl who crossed the wide sea
Carrying in my body the seed of the free.
I am the woman who worked in the field
Bringing the cotton and the corn to yield.
I am the one who labored as a slave,
Beaten and mistreated for the work that I gave—
Children sold away from me, husband sold, too.
No safety, no love, no respect was I due.
Three hundred years in the deepest South:
But God put a song and a prayer in my mouth.
God put a dream like steel in my soul.
Now, through my children, I'm reaching the goal.
Now, through my children, young and free,
I realize the blessings denied to me.
I couldn't read then. I couldn't write.
I had nothing, back there in the night.
Sometimes, the valley was filled with tears,
But I kept trudging on through the lonely years.
Sometimes, the road was hot with sun,
But I had to keep on till my work was done:

I *had* to keep on! No stopping for me—
I was the seed of the coming Free.
I nourished the dream that nothing could smother
Deep in my breast—the Negro mother.
I had only hope then, but now through you,
Dark ones of today, my dreams must come true:
All you dark children in the world out there,
Remember my sweat, my pain, my despair.
Remember my years, heavy with sorrow—
And make of those years a torch for tomorrow.
Make of my past a road to the light
Out of the darkness, the ignorance, the night.
Lift high my banner out of the dust.
Stand like free men supporting my trust.
Believe in the right, let none push you back.
Remember the whip and the slaver's track.
Remember how the strong in struggle and strife
Still bar you the way, and deny you life—
But march ever forward, breaking down bars.
Look ever upward at the sun and the stars.
Oh, my dark children, may my dreams and my prayers
Impel you forever up the great stairs—
For I will be with you till no white brother
Dares keep down the children of the Negro mother.

Good Morning Revolution

Good-morning, Revolution:
    You're the very best friend
    I ever had.
We gonna pal around together from now on.
Say, listen, Revolution:
You know, the boss where I used to work,
The guy that gimme the air to cut down expenses,
He wrote a long letter to the papers about you:
Said you was a trouble maker, a alien-enemy,
In other words a son-of-a-bitch.
He called up the police
And told 'em to watch out for a guy
Named Revolution.

You see,
The boss knows you're my friend.
He sees us hangin' out together.
He knows we're hungry, and ragged,
And ain't got a damn thing in this world—
And are gonna do something about it.

The boss's got all he needs, certainly,
    Eats swell,
    Owns a lotta houses,
    Goes vacationin',
    Breaks strikes,
    Runs politics, bribes police,

Pays off congress,
And struts all over the earth—

But me, I ain't never had enough to eat.
Me, I ain't never been warm in winter.
Me, I ain't never known security—
All my life, been livin' hand to mouth,
     Hand to mouth.

Listen, Revolution,
     We're buddies, see—
     Together,
     We can take everything:
     Factories, arsenals, houses, ships,
     Railroads, forests, fields, orchards,
     Bus lines, telegraphs, radios,
     (Jesus! Raise hell with radios!)
     Steel mills, coal mines, oil wells, gas,
     All the tools of production,
     (Great day in the morning!)
     Everything—
     And turn 'em over to the people who work.
     Rule and run 'em for us people who work.

Boy! Them radios—
Broadcasting that very first morning to USSR:
Another member the International Soviet's done come
Greetings to the Socialist Soviet Republics
Hey you rising workers everywhere greetings—
     And we'll sign it: *Germany*
     Sign it: *China*

Sign it: *Africa*
Sign it: *Poland*
Sign it: *Italy*
Sign it: *America*
Sign it with my one name: *Worker*
On that day when no one will be hungry, cold, oppressed,
Anywhere in the world again.

That's our job!

I been starvin' too long,
Ain't you?

Let's go, Revolution!

Share-Croppers

Just a herd of Negroes
Driven to the field,
Plowing, planting, hoeing,
To make the cotton yield.

When the cotton's picked
And the work is done
Boss man takes the money
And we get none,

Leaves us hungry, ragged
As we were before.
Year by year goes by
And we are nothing more

Than a herd of Negroes
Driven to the field—
Plowing life away
To make the cotton yield.

Let America Be America Again

Let America be America again.
Let it be the dream it used to be.
Let it be the pioneer on the plain
Seeking a home where he himself is free.

(America never was America to me.)

Let America be the dream the dreamers dreamed—
Let it be that great strong land of love
Where never kings connive nor tyrants scheme
That any man be crushed by one above.

(It never was America to me.)

O, let my land be a land where Liberty
Is crowned with no false patriotic wreath,

But opportunity is real, and life is free,
Equality is in the air we breathe.

(There's never been equality for me,
Nor freedom in this "homeland of the free.")

Say, who are you that mumbles in the dark?
And who are you that draws your veil across the stars?

I am the poor white, fooled and pushed apart,
I am the Negro bearing slavery's scars.
I am the red man driven from the land,
I am the immigrant clutching the hope I seek—
And finding only the same old stupid plan
Of dog eat dog, of mighty crush the weak.

I am the young man, full of strength and hope,
Tangled in that ancient endless chain
Of profit, power, gain, of grab the land!
Of grab the gold! Of grab the ways of satisfying need!
Of work the men! Of take the pay!
Of owning everything for one's own greed!

I am the farmer, bondsman to the soil.
I am the worker sold to the machine.
I am the Negro, servant to you all.
I am the people, humble, hungry, mean—
Hungry yet today despite the dream.
Beaten yet today—O, Pioneers!
I am the man who never got ahead,
The poorest worker bartered through the years.

Yet I'm the one who dreamt our basic dream
In that Old World while still a serf of kings,
Who dreamt a dream so strong, so brave, so true,
That even yet its mighty daring sings
In every brick and stone, in every furrow turned
That's made America the land it has become.
O, I'm the man who sailed those early seas
In search of what I meant to be my home—
For I'm the one who left dark Ireland's shore,
And Poland's plain, and England's grassy lea,
And torn from Black Africa's strand I came
To build a "homeland of the free."

The free?

Who said the free? Not me?
Surely not me? The millions on relief today?
The millions shot down when we strike?
The millions who have nothing for our pay?
For all the dreams we've dreamed
And all the songs we've sung
And all the hopes we've held
And all the flags we've hung,
The millions who have nothing for our pay—
Except the dream that's almost dead today.

O, let America be America again—
The land that never has been yet—
And yet must be—the land where *every* man is free.
The land that's mine—the poor man's, Indian's, Negro's, ME—

Who made America,
Whose sweat and blood, whose faith and pain,
Whose hand at the foundry, whose plow in the rain,
Must bring back our mighty dream again.

Sure, call me any ugly name you choose—
The steel of freedom does not stain.
From those who live like leeches on the people's lives,
We must take back our land again,
America!

O, yes,
I say it plain,
America never was America to me,
And yet I swear this oath—
America will be!

Out of the rack and ruin of our gangster death,
The rape and rot of graft, and stealth, and lies,
We, the people, must redeem
The land, the mines, the plants, the rivers.
The mountains and the endless plain—
All, all the stretch of these great green states—
And make America again!

In Time of Silver Rain

In time of silver rain
The earth
Puts forth new life again,
Green grasses grow
And flowers lift their heads,
And over all the plain
The wonder spreads
    Of life,
    Of life,
    Of life!

In time of silver rain
The butterflies
Lift silken wings
To catch a rainbow cry,
And trees put forth
New leaves to sing
In joy beneath the sky
As down the roadway
Passing boys and girls
Go singing, too,
In time of silver rain
    When spring
    And life
    Are new.

Daybreak in Alabama

When I get to be a composer
I'm gonna write me some music about
Daybreak in Alabama
And I'm gonna put the purtiest songs in it
Rising out of the ground like a swamp mist
And falling out of heaven like soft dew.
I'm gonna put some tall tall trees in it
And the scent of pine needles
And the smell of red clay after rain
And long red necks
And poppy colored faces
And big brown arms
And the field daisy eyes
Of black and white black white black people
And I'm gonna put white hands
And black hands and brown and yellow hands
And red clay earth hands in it
Touching everybody with kind fingers
And touching each other natural as dew
In that dawn of music when I
Get to be a composer
And write about daybreak
In Alabama.

Comment on War

Let us kill off youth
For the sake of *truth*.

We who are old know what truth is—
Truth is a bundle of vicious lies
Tied together and sterilized—
A war-makers' bait for unwise youth
To kill off each other
For the sake of
Truth.

Black Maria

Must be the Black Maria
That I see,
The Black Maria that I see—
But I hope it
Ain't comin' for me.

Hear that music playin' upstairs?
Aw, my heart is
Full of cares—
But that music playin' upstairs
Is for me.

Babe, did you ever
See the sun
Rise at dawnin' full of fun?
Says, did you ever see the sun rise
Full of fun, full of fun?
Then you know a new day's
Done begun.

Black Maria passin' by
Leaves the sunrise in the sky—
And a new day,
Yes, a new day's
Done begun!

Heaven

Heaven is
The place where
Happiness is
Everywhere.

Snail

Little snail,
Dreaming you go.

Weather and rose
Is all you know.

Weather and rose
Is all you see,
Drinking
The dewdrop's
Mystery.

Me and the Mule

My old mule,
He's got a grin on his face.
He's been a mule so long
He's forgot about his race.

I'm like that old mule—
Black—and don't give a damn!
You got to take me
Like I am.

Merry-Go-Round
Colored child at carnival

Where is the Jim Crow section
On this merry-go-round,

Mister, cause I want to ride?
Down South where I come from
White and colored
Can't sit side by side.
Down South on the train
There's a Jim Crow car.
On the bus we're put in the back—
But there ain't no back
To a merry-go-round!
Where's the horse
For a kid that's black?

The Bitter River

*(Dedicated to the memory of Charlie Lang and Ernest
Green, each fourteen years old when lynched together
beneath the Shubuta Bridge over the Chicasawhay River
in Mississippi, October 12th, 1942.)*

There is a bitter river
Flowing through the South.
Too long has the taste of its water
Been in my mouth.
There is a bitter river
Dark with filth and mud.
Too long has its evil poison
Poisoned my blood.

I've drunk of the bitter river
And its gall coats the red of my tongue,

Mixed with the blood of the lynched boys
From its iron bridge hung,
Mixed with the hopes that are drowned there
In the snake-like hiss of its stream
Where I drank of the bitter river
That strangled my dream:
The book studied—but useless,
Tool handled—but unused,
Knowledge acquired but thrown away,
Ambition battered and bruised.
Oh, water of the bitter river
With your taste of blood and clay,
You reflect no stars by night,
No sun by day.

The bitter river reflects no stars—
It gives back only the glint of steel bars
And dark bitter faces behind steel bars:
The Scottsboro boys behind steel bars,
Lewis Jones behind steel bars,
The voteless share-cropper behind steel bars,
The labor leader behind steel bars,
The soldier thrown from a Jim Crow bus behind steel bars,
The 15¢ mugger behind steel bars,
The girl who sells her body behind steel bars,
And my grandfather's back with its ladder of scars,
Long ago, long ago—the whip and steel bars—
The bitter river reflects no stars.

"Wait, be patient," you say.
"Your folks will have a better day."

But the swirl of the bitter river
Takes your words away.
"Work, education, patience
Will bring a better day."
The swirl of the bitter river
Carries your "patience" away.
"Disrupter! Agitator!
Trouble maker!" you say.

The swirl of the bitter river
Sweeps your lies away.
I did not ask for this river
Nor the taste of its bitter brew.
I was given its water
As a gift from you.
Yours has been the power
To force my back to the wall
And make me drink of the bitter cup
Mixed with blood and gall.

You have lynched my comrades
Where the iron bridge crosses the stream,
Underpaid me for my labor,
And spit in the face of my dream.
You forced me to the bitter river
With the hiss of its snake-like song—
Now your words no longer have meaning—
I have drunk at the river too long:
Dreamer of dreams to be broken,
Builder of hopes to be smashed,
Loser from an empty pocket

Of my meagre cash,
Bitter bearer of burdens
And singer of weary song,
I've drunk at the bitter river
With its filth and its mud too long.
Tired now of the bitter river,
Tired now of the pat on the back,
Tired now of the steel bars
Because my face is black,
I'm tired of segregation,
Tired of filth and mud,
I've drunk of the bitter river
And it's turned to steel in my blood.

Oh, tragic bitter river
Where the lynched boys hung,
The gall of your bitter water
Coats my tongue.
The blood of your bitter water
For me gives back no stars.
I'm tired of the bitter river!
Tired of the bars!

Ku Klux

They took me out
To some lonesome place.
They said, "Do you believe
In the great white race?"

I said, "Mister,
To tell you the truth,
I'd believe in anything
If you'd just turn me loose."

The white man said, "Boy,
Can it be
You're a-standin' there
A-sassin' me?"

They hit me in the head
And knocked me down.
And then they kicked me
On the ground.

A klansman said, "Nigger,
Look me in the face—
And tell me you believe in
The great white race."

Ballad of the Fortune Teller

Madam could look in your hand—
Never seen you before—
And tell you more than
You'd want to know.

She could tell you about love,
And money, and such.
And she wouldn't
Charge you much.

A fellow came one day.
Madam took him in.
She treated him like
He was her kin.

Gave him money to gamble.
She gave him bread,
And let him sleep in her
Walnut bed.

Friends tried to tell her
Dave meant her no good.
Looks like she could've knowed it
If she only would.

He mistreated her terrible,
Beat her up bad.

Then went off and left her.
Stole all she had.

She tried to find out
What road he took.
There wasn't a trace
No way she looked.

That woman who could foresee
What *your* future meant,
Couldn't tell, to save her,
Where Dave went.

Ballad of the Gypsy

I went to the Gypsy's.
Gypsy settin' all alone.
I said, Tell me, Gypsy,
When will my gal be home?

Gypsy said, Silver,
Put some silver in my hand
And I'll look into the future
And tell you all I can.

I crossed her palm with silver,
Then she started in to lie.

She said, Now, listen, Mister,
She'll be here by and by.

   Aw, what a lie!

I been waitin' and a-waitin'
And she ain't come home yet.
Something musta happened
To make my gal forget.

Uh! I hates a lyin' Gypsy
Will take good money from you,
Tell you pretty stories
And take your money from you—

But if I was a Gypsy
I would take your money, too.

Widow Woman

Oh, that last long ride is a
Ride everybody must take.
Yes, that last long ride's a
Ride everybody must take.
And that final stop is a
Stop everybody must make.

When they put you in the ground and
They throw dirt in your face,
I say put you in the ground and
Throw dirt in your face,
That's one time, pretty papa,
You'll sure stay in your place.

You was a mighty lover and you
Ruled me many years.
A mighty lover, baby, cause you
Ruled me many years—
If I live to be a thousand
I'll never dry these tears.

I don't want nobody else and
Don't nobody else want me.
I say don't want nobody else
And don't nobody else want me—

Yet you never can tell when a
Woman like me is free!

Love

Love is a wild wonder
And stars that sing,
Rocks that burst asunder
And mountains that take wing.

John Henry with his hammer
Makes a little spark.
That little spark is love
Dying in the dark.

Freedom's Plow

When a man starts out with nothing,
When a man starts out with his hands
Empty, but clean,
When a man starts out to build a world,
He starts first with himself
And the faith that is in his heart—
The strength there,
The will there to build.

First in the heart is the dream.
Then the mind starts seeking a way.
His eyes look out on the world,
On the great wooded world,
On the rich soil of the world,
On the rivers of the world.

The eyes see there materials for building,
See the difficulties, too, and the obstacles.
The hand seeks tools to cut the wood,
To till the soil, and harness the power of the waters.

Then the hand seeks other hands to help,
A community of hands to help—
Thus the dream becomes not one man's dream alone,
But a community dream.
Not my dream alone, but *our* dream.
Not my world alone,
But *your world and my world,*
Belonging to all the hands who build.

A long time ago, but not too long ago,
Ships came from across the sea
Bringing Pilgrims and prayer-makers,
Adventurers and booty seekers,
Free men and indentured servants,
Slave men and slave masters, all new—
To a new world, America!

With billowing sails the galleons came
Bringing men and dreams, women and dreams.
In little bands together,
Heart reaching out to heart,
Hand reaching out to hand,
They began to build our land.
Some were free hands
Seeking a greater freedom,
Some were indentured hands
Hoping to find their freedom,
Some were slave hands
Guarding in their hearts the seed of freedom.
But the word was there always:
    FREEDOM.

Down into the earth went the plow
In the free hands and the slave hands,
In indentured hands and adventurous hands,
Turning the rich soil went the plow in many hands
That planted and harvested the food that fed
And the cotton that clothed America.
Clang against the trees went the ax in many hands
That hewed and shaped the rooftops of America.
Splash into the rivers and the seas went the boat-hulls
That moved and transported America.
Crack went the whips that drove the horses
Across the plains of America.
Free hands and slave hands,
Indentured hands, adventurous hands,
White hands and black hands
Held the plow handles,
Ax handles, hammer handles,
Launched the boats and whipped the horses
That fed and housed and moved America.
Thus together through labor,
All these hands made America.
Labor! Out of labor came the villages
And the towns that grew to cities.
Labor! Out of labor came the rowboats
And the sailboats and the steamboats,
Came the wagons, stage coaches,
Out of labor came the factories,
Came the foundries, came the railroads,
Came the marts and markets, shops and stores,
Came the mighty products moulded, manufactured,

Sold in shops, piled in warehouses,
Shipped the wide world over:
Out of labor—white hands and black hands—
Came the dream, the strength, the will,
And the way to build America.
Now it is Me here, and You there.
Now it's Manhattan, Chicago,
Seattle, New Orleans,
Boston and El Paso—
Now it is the U.S.A.

A long time ago, but not too long ago, a man said:

> ALL MEN ARE CREATED EQUAL . . .
> ENDOWED BY THEIR CREATOR
> WITH CERTAIN INALIENABLE
>   RIGHTS . . .
> AMONG THESE, LIFE, LIBERTY
> AND THE PURSUIT OF HAPPINESS.

His name was Jefferson. There were slaves then,
But in their hearts the slaves believed him, too,
And silently took for granted
That what he said was also meant for them.
It was a long time ago,
But not so long ago at that, Lincoln said:

> NO MAN IS GOOD ENOUGH
> TO GOVERN ANOTHER MAN
> WITHOUT THAT OTHER'S CONSENT.

There were slaves then, too,
But in their hearts the slaves knew
What he said must be meant for every human being—
Else it had no meaning for anyone.
Then a man said:

> BETTER TO DIE FREE,
> THAN TO LIVE SLAVES.

He was a colored man who had been a slave
But had run away to freedom.
And the slaves knew
What Frederick Douglass said was true.
With John Brown at Harpers Ferry, Negroes died.
John Brown was hung.
Before the Civil War, days were dark,
And nobody knew for sure
When freedom would triumph.
"Or if it would," thought some.
But others knew it had to triumph.
In those dark days of slavery,
Guarding in their hearts the seed of freedom,
The slaves made up a song:

> KEEP YOUR HAND ON THE PLOW!
> HOLD ON!

That song meant just what it said: *Hold on!*
Freedom will come!

KEEP YOUR HAND ON THE PLOW!
HOLD ON!

Out of war, it came, bloody and terrible!
But it came!
Some there were, as always,
Who doubted that the war would end right,
That the slaves would be free,
Or that the union would stand.
But now we know how it all came out.
Out of the darkest days for a people and a nation,
We know now how it came out.
There was light when the battle clouds rolled away.
There was a great wooded land,
And men united as a nation.

America is a dream.
The poet says it was promises.
The people say it *is* promises—that will come true.
The people do not always say things out loud,
Nor write them down on paper.
The people often hold
Great thoughts in their deepest hearts
And sometimes only blunderingly express them,
Haltingly and stumbling say them,
And faultily put them into practice.
The people do not always understand each other.
But there is, somewhere there,
Always the *trying* to understand,
And the *trying* to say,
"You are a man. Together we are building our land."

America!
Land created in common,
Dream nourished in common,
Keep your hand on the plow! Hold on!
If the house is not yet finished,
Don't be discouraged, builder!
If the fight is not yet won,
Don't be weary, soldier!
The plan and the pattern is here,
Woven from the beginning
Into the warp and woof of America:

 ALL MEN ARE CREATED EQUAL.

 NO MAN IS GOOD ENOUGH
 TO GOVERN ANOTHER MAN WITHOUT
 THAT OTHER'S CONSENT.

 BETTER DIE FREE,
 THAN LIVE SLAVES.

Who said those things? Americans!
Who owns those words? America!
Who is America? You, me!
We are America!
To the enemy who would conquer us from without,
We say, NO!
To the enemy who would divide
and conquer us from within,
We say, NO!

FREEDOM!
    BROTHERHOOD!
        DEMOCRACY!

To all the enemies of these great words:
We say, NO!

A long time ago,
An enslaved people heading toward freedom
Made up a song:
   Keep Your Hand On The Plow! Hold On!
That plow plowed a new furrow
Across the field of history.
Into that furrow the freedom seed was dropped.
From that seed a tree grew, is growing, will ever grow.
That tree is for everybody,
For all America, for all the world.
May its branches spread and its shelter grow
Until all races and all peoples know its shade.

    KEEP YOUR HAND ON THE PLOW!
      HOLD ON!

Words Like Freedom

There are words like *Freedom*
Sweet and wonderful to say.
On my heartstrings freedom sings
All day everyday.

There are words like *Liberty*
That almost make me cry.
If you had known what I know
You would know why.

Little Old Letter

It was yesterday morning
I looked in my box for mail.
The letter that I found there
Made me turn right pale.

Just a little old letter,
Wasn't even one page long—
But it made me wish
I was in my grave and gone.

I turned it over,
Not a word writ on the back.

I never felt so lonesome
Since I was born black.

Just a pencil and paper,
You don't need no gun nor knife—
A little old letter
Can take a person's life.

Madam and the Rent Man

The rent man knocked.
He said, Howdy-do?
I said, What
Can I do for you?
He said, You know
Your rent is due.

I said, Listen,
Before I'd pay
I'd go to Hades
And rot away!

The sink is broke,
The water don't run,
And you ain't done a thing
You promised to've done.

Back window's cracked,
Kitchen floor squeaks,
There's rats in the cellar,
And the attic leaks.

He said, Madam,
It's not up to me.
I'm just the agent,
Don't you see?

I said, Naturally,
You pass the buck.
If it's money you want
You're out of luck.

He said, Madam,
I ain't pleased!
I said, Neither am I.

So we agrees!

Madam and Her Madam

I worked for a woman,
She wasn't mean—
But she had a twelve-room
House to clean.

Had to get breakfast,
Dinner, and supper, too—
Then take care of her children
When I got through.

Wash, iron, and scrub,
Walk the dog around—
It was too much,
Nearly broke me down.

I said, Madam,
Can it be
You trying to make a
Pack-horse out of me?

She opened her mouth.
She cried, Oh, no!
You know, Alberta,
I love you so!

I said, Madam,
That may be true—
But I'll be dogged
If I love you!

Still Here

I've been scared and battered.
My hopes the wind done scattered.
Snow has friz me, sun has baked me.
Looks like between 'em
They done tried to make me
Stop laughin', stop lovin', stop livin'—
But I don't care!
I'm still here!

Madam's Past History

My name is Johnson—
Madam Alberta K.
The Madam stands for business.
I'm smart that way.

I had a
HAIR-DRESSING PARLOR
Before
The depression put
The prices lower.

Then I had a
BARBECUE STAND

Till I got mixed up
With a no-good man.

Cause I had a insurance
The WPA
Said, We can't use you
Wealthy that way.

I said,
DON'T WORRY 'BOUT ME!
Just like the song,
You WPA folks take care of yourself—
And I'll get along.

I do cooking,
Day's work, too!
Alberta K. Johnson—
Madam to you.

I Dream a World

I dream a world where man
No other man will scorn,
Where love will bless the earth
And peace its paths adorn.
I dream a world where all
Will know sweet freedom's way,
Where greed no longer saps the soul

Nor avarice blights our day.
A world I dream where black or white,
Whatever race you be,
Will share the bounties of the earth
And every man is free,
Where wretchedness will hang its head
And joy, like a pearl,
Attends the needs of all mankind—
Of such I dream, my world!

The Heart of Harlem

The buildings in Harlem are brick and stone
And the streets are long and wide,
But Harlem's much more than these alone,
Harlem is what's inside—
It's a song with a minor refrain,
It's a dream you keep dreaming again.
It's a tear you turn into a smile.
It's the sunrise you know is coming after a while.
It's the shoes that you get half-soled twice.
It's the kid you hope will grow up nice.
It's the hand that's working all day long.
It's a prayer that keeps you going along—
        That's the Heart of Harlem!

It's Joe Louis and Dr. W. E. B.,
A stevedore, a porter, Marian Anderson, and me.

It's Father Divine and the music of Earl Hines,
Adam Powell in Congress, our drivers on bus lines.
It's Dorothy Maynor and it's Billie Holiday,
The lectures at the Schomburg and the Apollo down the way.
It's Father Shelton Bishop and shouting Mother Horne.
It's the Rennie and the Savoy where new dances are born.
It's Canada Lee's penthouse at Five-Fifty-Five.
It's Small's Paradise and Jimmy's little dive.
It's 409 Edgecombe or a cold-water walk-up flat—
But it's where I live and it's where my love is at
        Deep in the Heart of Harlem!

It's the pride all Americans know.
It's the faith God gave us long ago.
It's the strength to make our dreams come true.
It's a feeling warm and friendly given to you.
It's that girl with the rhythmical walk.
It's my boy with the jive in his talk.
It's the man with the muscles of steel.
It's the right to be free a people never will yield.
A dream . . . a song . . . half-soled shoes . . . dancing shoes
A tear . . . a smile . . . the blues . . . sometimes the blues
Mixed with the memory . . . and forgiveness . . . of our wrong.
But more than that, it's freedom—
Guarded for the kids who came along—
        Folks, that's the Heart of Harlem!

Graduation

Cinnamon and rayon,
Jet and coconut eyes,
Mary Lulu Jackson
Smooths the skirt
At her thighs.

Mama, portly oven,
Brings remainders from the kitchen
Where the people all are icebergs
Wrapped in checks and wealthy.

𝔇iploma in its new frame:
Mary Lulu Jackson
Eating chicken,
Tells her mama she's a typist
And the clicking of the keys
Will spell the name
Of a job in a fine office
Far removed from basic oven,
Cookstoves,
And iceberg's kitchen.

Mama says, *Praise Jesus!*
Until then
I'll bring home chicken!

The 𝔇iploma bursts its frame
To scatter star-dust in their eyes.

Mama says, *Praise Jesus!*
The colored race will rise!

Mama says,
Praise Jesus!

Then,
Because she's tired,
She sighs.

Who but the Lord?

I looked and I saw
That man they call the Law.
He was coming
Down the street at me!
I had visions in my head
Of being laid out cold and dead,
Or else murdered
By the third degree.

I said, *O, Lord, if you can,*
Save me from that man!
Don't let him make a pulp out of me!
But the Lord he was not quick.
The Law raised up his stick

And beat the living hell
Out of me!

Now I do not understand
Why God don't protect a man
From police brutality.
Being poor and black,
I've no weapon to strike back
So who but the Lord
Can protect me?

    We'll see.

Freedom Train

     I read in the papers about the
         Freedom Train.
     I heard on the radio about the
         Freedom Train.
     I seen folks talkin' about the
         Freedom Train.
     Lord, I been a-waitin' for the
         Freedom Train!

Down South in Dixie only train I see's
Got a Jim Crow car set aside for me.
I hope there ain't no Jim Crow on the Freedom Train,

No back door entrance to the Freedom Train,
No signs FOR COLORED on the Freedom Train,
No WHITE FOLKS ONLY on the Freedom Train.

    I'm gonna check up on this
        Freedom Train.

Who's the engineer on the Freedom Train?
Can a coal black man drive the Freedom Train?
Or am I still a porter on the Freedom Train?
Is there ballot boxes on the Freedom Train?
When it stops in Mississippi will it be made plain
Everybody's got a right to board the Freedom Train?

    Somebody tell me about this
        Freedom Train!

The Birmingham station's marked COLORED and WHITE.
The white folks go left, the colored go right—
They even got a segregated lane.
Is that the way to get aboard the Freedom Train?

    I got to know about this
        Freedom Train!

If my children ask me, *Daddy, please explain*
Why there's Jim Crow stations for the Freedom Train?
What shall I tell my children? . . . *You* tell me—
'Cause freedom ain't freedom when a man ain't free.

But maybe they explains it on the
    Freedom Train.

When my grandmother in Atlanta, 83 and black,
Gets in line to see the Freedom,
Will some white man yell, *Get back!*
A Negro's got no business on the Freedom Track!

    Mister, I thought it were the
      Freedom Train!

Her grandson's name was Jimmy. He died at Anzio.
He died for real. It warn't no show.
The freedom that they carryin' on this Freedom Train,
Is it for real—or just a show again?

    Jimmy wants to know about the
      Freedom Train.

Will *his* Freedom Train come zoomin' down the track
Gleamin' in the sunlight for white and black?
Not stoppin' at no stations marked COLORED nor WHITE,
Just stoppin' in the fields in the broad daylight,
Stoppin' in the country in the wide-open air
Where there never was no Jim Crow signs nowhere,
No Welcomin' Committees, nor politicians of note,
No Mayors and such for which colored can't vote,
And nary a sign of a color line—
For the Freedom Train will be yours and mine!

Then maybe from their graves in Anzio
The G.I.'s who fought will say, *We wanted it so!*
Black men and white will say, *Ain't it fine?*
At home they got a train that's yours and mine!

> Then I'll shout, *Glory for the*
> > *Freedom Train!*
> I'll holler, *Blow your whistle,*
> > *Freedom Train!*
> *Thank God-A-Mighty! Here's the*
> > *Freedom Train!*
> *Get on board our Freedom Train!*

End

There are
No clocks on the wall,
And no time,
No shadows that move
From dawn to dusk
Across the floor.

There is neither light
Nor dark
Outside the door.

There is no door!

Fulfillment

The earth-meaning
Like the sky-meaning
Was fulfilled.

We got up
And went to the river,
Touched silver water,
Laughed and bathed
In the sunshine.

Day
Became a bright ball of light
For us to play with,
Sunset
A yellow curtain,
Night
A velvet screen.

The moon,
Like an old grandmother,
Blessed us with a kiss
And sleep
Took us both in
Laughing.

Dream Dust

Gather out of star-dust,
    Earth-dust,
    Cloud-dust,
    Storm-dust,
And splinters of hail,
One handful of dream-dust
    Not for sale.

Trumpet Player

The Negro
With the trumpet at his lips
Has dark moons of weariness
Beneath his eyes
Where the smoldering memory
Of slave ships
Blazed to the crack of whips
About his thighs.

The Negro
With the trumpet at his lips
Has a head of vibrant hair
Tamed down,
Patent-leathered now
Until it gleams

Like jet—
Were jet a crown.

The music
From the trumpet at his lips
Is honey
Mixed with liquid fire.
The rhythm
From the trumpet at his lips
Is ecstasy
Distilled from old desire—

Desire
That is longing for the moon
Where the moonlight's but a spotlight
In his eyes,
Desire
That is longing for the sea
Where the sea's a bar-glass
Sucker size.

The Negro
With the trumpet at his lips
Whose jacket
Has a *fine* one-button roll,
Does not know
Upon what riff the music slips
Its hypodermic needle
To his soul—

But softly
As the tune comes from his throat
Trouble
Mellows to a golden note.

Madam and the Census Man

The census man,
The day he came round,
Wanted my name
To put it down.

I said, JOHNSON,
ALBERTA K.
But he hated to write
The K that way.

He said, What
Does K stand for?
I said, K—
And nothing more.

He said, I'm gonna put it
K—A—Y.
I said, If you do,
You lie.

My mother christened me
ALBERTA K.
You leave my name
Just that way!

He said, Mrs.,
(With a snort)
Just a K
Makes your name too short.

I said, I don't
Give a damn!
Leave me and my name
Just like I am!

Furthermore, rub out
That MRS., too—
I'll have you know
I'm *Madam* to you!

Mama and Daughter

Mama, please brush off my coat.
I'm going down the street.

Where're you going, daughter?

To see my sugar-sweet.

Who is your sugar, honey?
Turn around—I'll brush behind.

> *He is that young man, mama,*
> *I can't get off my mind.*

Daughter, once upon a time—
Let me brush the hem—
Your father, yes, he was the one!
I felt like that about him.

But it was a long time ago
He up and went his way.
I hope that wild young son-of-a-gun
Rots in hell today!

> *Mama, dad couldn't be still young.*

He *was* young yesterday.
He *was* young when he—
Turn around!
So I can brush your back, I say!

Life Is Fine

I went down to the river,
I set down on the bank.

I tried to think but couldn't,
So I jumped in and sank.

I came up once and hollered!
I came up twice and cried!
If that water hadn't a-been so cold
I might've sunk and died.

> *But it was*
> *Cold in that water!*
> *It was cold!*

I took the elevator
Sixteen floors above the ground.
I thought about my baby
And thought I would jump down.

I stood there and I hollered!
I stood there and I cried!
If it hadn't a-been so high
I might've jumped and died.

> *But it was*
> *High up there!*
> *It was high!*

So since I'm still here livin',
I guess I will live on.
I could've died for love—
But for livin' I was born.

Though you may hear me holler,
And you may see me cry—
I'll be dogged, sweet baby,
If you gonna see me die.

> *Life is fine!*
> *Fine as wine!*
> *Life is fine!*

Song for Billie Holiday

What can purge my heart
    Of the song
    And the sadness?
What can purge my heart
    But the song
    Of the sadness?
What can purge my heart
    Of the sadness
    Of the song?

Do not speak of sorrow
With dust in her hair,
Or bits of dust in eyes
A chance wind blows there.
The sorrow that I speak of
Is dusted with despair.

Voice of muted trumpet,
Cold brass in warm air.
Bitter television blurred
By sound that shimmers—
        Where?

Late Last Night

Late last night I
Set on my steps and cried.
Wasn't nobody gone,
Neither had nobody died.

I was cryin'
Cause you broke my heart in two.
You looked at me cross-eyed
And broke my heart in two—

So I was cryin'
On account of
You!

Could Be

Could be Hastings Street,
Or Lenox Avenue,
Could be 18th & Vine
And still be true.

Could be 5th & Mound,
Could be Rampart:
When you pawned my watch
You pawned my heart.

Could be you love me,
Could be that you don't.
Might be that you'll come back,
Like as not you won't.

Hastings Street is weary,
Also Lenox Avenue.
Any place is dreary
Without my watch and you.

Midnight Raffle

I put my nickel
In the raffle of the night.

Somehow that raffle
Didn't turn out right.

I lost my nickel.
I lost my time.
I got back home
Without a dime.

When I dropped that nickel
In the subway slot,
I wouldn't have dropped it,
Knowing what I got.

I could just as well've
Stayed home inside:
My bread wasn't buttered
On neither side.

Final Curve

When you turn the corner
And you run into *yourself*
Then you know that you have turned
All the corners that are left.

To Be Somebody

Little girl
Dreaming of a baby grand piano
(Not knowing there's a Steinway bigger, bigger)
Dreaming of a baby grand to play
That stretches paddle-tailed across the floor,
Not standing upright
Like a bad boy in the corner,
But sending music
Up the stairs and down the stairs
And out the door
To confound even Hazel Scott
Who might be passing!

Oh!

Little boy
Dreaming of the boxing gloves
Joe Louis wore,
The gloves that sent
Two dozen men to the floor.
Knockout!
Bam! Bop! Mop!

There's always room,
They say,
At the top.

Kid in the Park

Lonely little question mark
on a bench in the park:

See the people passing by?
See the airplanes in the sky?
See the birds
flying home
before
dark?

Home's just around
the corner
there—
but not really
anywhere.

Dream Boogie

Good morning, daddy!
Ain't you heard
The boogie-woogie rumble
Of a dream deferred?

Listen closely:
You'll hear their feet
Beating out and beating out a—

> *You think*
> *It's a happy beat?*

Listen to it closely:
Ain't you heard
something underneath
like a—

> *What did I say?*

Sure,
I'm happy!
Take it away!

> *Hey, pop!*
> *Re-bop!*
> *Mop!*

> *Y-e-a-h!*

Preference

I likes a woman
six or eight or ten years older'n myself.

I don't fool with these young girls.
Young girl'll say,
        Daddy, I want so-and-so.
        I needs this, that, and the other.
But a old woman'll say,
        Honey, what does YOU need?
        I just drawed my money tonight
        and it's all your'n.
That's why I likes a older woman
who can appreciate me:
When she conversations you
it ain't forever, *Gimme!*

Juke Box Love Song

I could take the Harlem night
and wrap around you,
Take the neon lights and make a crown,
Take the Lenox Avenue busses,
Taxis, subways,
And for your love song tone their rumble down.
Take Harlem's heartbeat,
Make a drumbeat,
Put it on a record, let it whirl,
And while we listen to it play,
Dance with you till day—
Dance with you, my sweet brown Harlem girl.

Easy Boogie

Down in the bass
That steady beat
Walking walking walking
Like marching feet.

Down in the bass
That easy roll,
Rolling like I like it
In my soul.

     Riffs, smears, breaks.

Hey, Lawdy, Mama!
Do you hear what I said?
Easy like I rock it
In my bed!

Dead in There

Sometimes
A night funeral
Going by
Carries home
A cool bop daddy.

Hearse and flowers
Guarantee
He'll never hype
Another paddy.

It's hard to believe,
But dead in there,
He'll never lay a
Hype nowhere!

He's my ace-boy,
Gone away.
Wake up and live!
He used to say.

Squares
Who couldn't dig him,
Plant him now—
Out where it makes
No diff' no how.

Advice

Folks, I'm telling you,
birthing is hard
and dying is mean—
so get yourself
a little loving
in between.

Ballad of the Landlord

Landlord, landlord,
My roof has sprung a leak.
Don't you 'member I told you about it
Way last week?

Landlord, landlord,
These steps is broken down.
When you come up yourself
It's a wonder you don't fall down.

Ten Bucks you say I owe you?
Ten Bucks you say is due?
Well, that's Ten Bucks more'n I'll pay you
Till you fix this house up new.

What? You gonna get eviction orders?
You gonna cut off my heat?
You gonna take my furniture and
Throw it in the street?

Um-huh! You talking high and mighty.
Talk on—till you get through.
You ain't gonna be able to say a word
If I land my fist on you.

Police! Police!
Come and get this man!
He's trying to ruin the government
And overturn the land!

Copper's whistle!
Patrol bell!
Arrest.

Precinct Station.
Iron cell.
Headlines in press:

MAN THREATENS LANDLORD
•
•   •

TENANT HELD NO BAIL
•
•   •

JUDGE GIVES NEGRO 90 DAYS IN COUNTY JAIL.

Projection

On the day when the Savoy
leaps clean over to Seventh Avenue
and starts jitterbugging
with the Renaissance,
on that day when Abyssinia Baptist Church
throws her enormous arms around
St. James Presbyterian
and 409 Edgecombe
stoops to kiss 12 West 133rd,
on that day—
Do, Jesus!
Manhattan Island will whirl
like a Dizzy Gillespie transcription
played by Inez and Timme.
On that day, Lord,
Sammy Davis and Marian Anderson
will sing a duet,
Paul Robeson
will team up with Jackie Mabley,
and Father Divine will say in truth,

> *Peace!*
> *It's truly*
> *wonderful!*

Drunkard

Voice grows thicker
as song grows stronger
as time grows longer until day
trying to forget to remember
the taste of day.

125th Street

Face like a chocolate bar
full of nuts and sweet.

Face like a jack-o'-lantern,
candle inside.

Face like a slice of melon,
grin that wide.

Theme for English B

The instructor said,

> *Go home and write*
> *a page tonight.*
> *And let that page come out of you—*
> *Then, it will be true.*

I wonder if it's that simple?
I am twenty-two, colored, born in Winston-Salem.
I went to school there, then Durham, then here
to this college on the hill above Harlem.
I am the only colored student in my class.
The steps from the hill lead down into Harlem,
through a park, then I cross St. Nicholas,
Eighth Avenue, Seventh, and I come to the Y,
the Harlem Branch Y, where I take the elevator
up to my room, sit down, and write this page:

It's not easy to know what is true for you or me
at twenty-two, my age. But I guess I'm what
I feel and see and hear, Harlem, I hear you:
hear you, hear me—we two—you, me, talk on this page.
(I hear New York, too.) Me—who?
Well, I like to eat, sleep, drink, and be in love.
I like to work, read, learn, and understand life.
I like a pipe for a Christmas present,
or records—Bessie, bop, or Bach.
I guess being colored doesn't make me *not* like

the same things other folks like who are other races.
So will my page be colored that I write?
Being me, it will not be white.
But it will be
a part of you, instructor.
You are white—
yet a part of me, as I am a part of you.
That's American.
Sometimes perhaps you don't want to be a part of me.
Nor do I often want to be a part of you.
But we are, that's true!
As I learn from you,
I guess you learn from me—
although you're older—and white—
and somewhat more free.

This is my page for English B.

College Formal: Renaissance Casino

Golden girl
in a golden gown
in a melody night
in Harlem town
lad tall and brown
tall and wise
college boy smart
eyes in eyes

the music wraps
them both around
in mellow magic
of dancing sound
till they're the heart
of the whole big town
gold and brown

Boogie: 1 A.M.

Good evening, daddy!
I know you've heard
The boogie-woogie rumble
Of a dream deferred
Trilling the treble
And twining the bass
Into midnight ruffles
Of cat-gut lace.

Lady's Boogie

See that lady
Dressed so fine?
She ain't got boogie-woogie
On her mind—

But if she was to listen
I bet she'd hear,
Way up in the treble
The tingle of a tear.

    Be-Bach!

World War II

What a grand time was the war!
    Oh, my, my!
What a grand time was the war!
    My, my, my!
In wartime we had fun,
Sorry that old war is done!
What a grand time was the war,
    My, my!

Echo:
    Did
    Somebody
    Die?

Mystery

When a chile gets to be thirteen
and ain't seen Christ yet,
she needs to set on de moaner's bench
night and day.

Jesus, lover of my soul!

Hail, Mary, mother of God!

Let me to thy bosom fly!

Amen! Hallelujah!

Swing low, sweet chariot,
Coming for to carry me home.

Sunday morning where the rhythm flows,
how old nobody knows—
yet old as mystery,
older than creed,
basic and wondering
and lost as my need.

> *Eli, eli!*

> *Te deum!*

> *Mahomet!*

Christ!

Father Bishop, Effendi, Mother Horne,
Father Divine, a Rabbi black
as black was born,
a jack-leg preacher, a Ph.D.

> *The mystery*
> *and the darkness*
> *and the song*
> *and me.*

Passing

On sunny summer Sunday afternoons in Harlem
when the air is one interminable ball game
and grandma cannot get her gospel hymns
from the Saints of God in Christ
on account of the Dodgers on the radio,
on sunny Sunday afternoons
when the kids look all new
and far too clean to stay that way,
and Harlem has its
washed-and-ironed-and-cleaned-best out,
the ones who've crossed the line
to live downtown
miss you,

Harlem of the bitter dream,
since their dream has
come true.

Nightmare Boogie

I had a dream
and I could see
a million faces
black as me!
A nightmare dream:
Quicker than light
All them faces
Turned dead white!
Boogie-woogie,
Rolling bass,
Whirling treble
of cat-gut lace.

Harlem [2]

What happens to a dream deferred?

　　Does it dry up
　　like a raisin in the sun?

Or fester like a sore—
And then run?
Does it stink like rotten meat?
Or crust and sugar over—
like a syrupy sweet?

Maybe it just sags
like a heavy load.

Or does it explode?

Good Morning

Good morning, daddy!
I was born here, he said,
watched Harlem grow
until colored folks spread
from river to river
across the middle of Manhattan
out of Penn Station
dark tenth of a nation,
planes from Puerto Rico,
and holds of boats, chico,
up from Cuba Haiti Jamaica,
in buses marked New York
from Georgia Florida Louisiana
to Harlem Brooklyn the Bronx
but most of all to Harlem

dusky sash across Manhattan
I've seen them come dark
    wondering
    wide-eyed
    dreaming
out of Penn Station—
but the trains are late.
The gates open—
       Yet there're bars
      at each gate.

       What happens
       to a dream deferred?

     Daddy, ain't you heard?

Same in Blues

I said to my baby,
Baby, take it slow.
I can't, she said, I can't!
I got to go!

   There's a certain
   amount of traveling
   in a dream deferred.

Lulu said to Leonard,
I want a diamond ring.
Leonard said to Lulu,
You won't get a goddamn thing!

> *A certain*
> *amount of nothing*
> *in a dream deferred.*

Daddy, daddy, daddy,
All I want is you.
You can have me, baby—
but my lovin' days is through.

> *A certain*
> *amount of impotence*
> *in a dream deferred.*

Three parties
On my party line—
But that third party,
Lord, ain't mine!

> *There's liable*
> *to be confusion*
> *in a dream deferred.*

From river to river,
Uptown and down,
There's liable to be confusion
when a dream gets kicked around.

Island [2]

Between two rivers
North of the park,
Like darker rivers
The streets are dark.

Black and white,
Gold and brown—
Chocolate-custard
Pie of a town.

Dream within a dream,
Our dream deferred.

Good morning, daddy!

Ain't you heard?

Bible Belt

It would be too bad if Jesus
Were to come back black.
There are so many churches
Where he could not pray
In the U.S.A.,
Where entrance to Negroes,

No matter how sanctified,
Is denied,
Where race, not religion,
Is glorified.
But say it—
You may be
Crucified.

Africa

Sleepy giant,
You've been resting awhile.
Now I see the thunder
And the lightning
In your smile.
Now I see
The storm clouds
In your waking eyes:
The thunder,
The wonder,
And the young
Surprise.
Your every step reveals
The new stride
In your thighs.

Without Benefit of Declaration

Listen here, Joe,
Don't you know
That tomorrow
You got to go
Out yonder where
The steel winds blow?

Listen here, kid,
It's been said
Tomorrow you'll be dead
Out there where
The rain is lead.

Don't ask me why.
Just go ahead and die.
Hidden from the sky
Out yonder you'll lie:
A medal to your family—
In exchange for
     A guy.

Mama, don't cry.

Georgia Dusk

Sometimes there's a wind in the Georgia dusk
That cries and cries and cries
Its lonely pity through the Georgia dusk
Veiling what the darkness hides.

Sometimes there's blood in the Georgia dusk,
Left by a streak of sun,
A crimson trickle in the Georgia dusk.
Whose blood? . . . Everyone's.

Sometimes a wind in the Georgia dusk
Scatters hate like seed
To sprout its bitter barriers
Where the sunsets bleed.

Mississippi

Oh, what sorrow!
Oh, what pity!
Oh, what pain
That tears and blood
Should mix like rain
And terror come again
To Mississippi.

Again?
Where has terror been?
On vacation? Up North?
In some other section
Of the Nation,
Lying low, unpublicized,
Masked—with only
Jaundiced eyes showing
Through the mask?

What sorrow, pity, pain,
That tears and blood
Still mix like rain
In Mississippi!

Where? When? Which?

When the cold comes
With a bitter fragrance
Like rusty iron and mint,
And the wind blows
Sharp as integration
With an edge like apartheid,
And it is winter,
And the cousins of the too-thin suits
Ride on bitless horses
Tethered by something worse than pride,
Which areaway, or bar,

Or station waiting room
Will not say,
Horse and horseman, outside!
With old and not too gentle
Apartheid?

To Artina

I will take your heart.
I will take your soul out of your body
As though I were God.
I will not be satisfied
With the little words you say to me.
I will not be satisfied
With the touch of your hand
Nor the sweet of your lips alone.
I will take your heart for mine.
I will take your soul.
I will be God when it comes to you.

Cultural Exchange

IN THE   *The*
IN THE QUARTER   *rhythmically*
IN THE QUARTER OF THE NEGROES   *rough*

WHERE THE DOORS ARE DOORS OF PAPER   *scraping*

DUST OF DINGY ATOMS   *of a guira*

BLOWS A SCRATCHY SOUND.   *continues*

AMORPHOUS JACK-O'-LANTERNS CAPER   *monotonously*

AND THE WIND WON'T WAIT FOR MIDNIGHT   *until a lonely*

FOR FUN TO BLOW DOORS DOWN.   *flute call,*

                                          high and

BY THE RIVER AND THE RAILROAD   *far away,*

WITH FLUID FAR-OFF GOING   *merges*

BOUNDARIES BIND UNBINDING   *into piano*

A WHIRL OF WHISTLES BLOWING   *variations*

NO TRAINS OR STEAMBOATS GOING   *on German*

YET LEONTYNE'S UNPACKING.   *lieder*

                                          gradually

IN THE QUARTER OF THE NEGROES   *changing*

WHERE THE DOORKNOB LETS IN LIEDER   *into*

MORE THAN GERMAN EVER BORE,   *old-time*

HER YESTERDAY PAST GRANDPA—   *traditional*

NOT OF HER OWN DOING—   *12-bar*

IN A POT OF COLLARD GREENS   *blues*

IS GENTLY STEWING.   *up strong*

                                          between verses

THERE, FORBID US TO REMEMBER,   *until*

COMES AN AFRICAN IN MID-DECEMBER   *African*

SENT BY THE STATE DEPARTMENT   *drums*

AMONG THE SHACKS TO MEET THE BLACKS: *throb*

LEONTYNE SAMMY HARRY POITIER   *against*

LOVELY LENA MARIAN LOUIS PEARLIE MAE   *blues*

GEORGE S. SCHUYLER MOLTO BENE   *fading*

COME WHAT MAY LANGSTON HUGHES   *as the*

IN THE QUARTER OF THE NEGROES   *music*
WHERE THE RAILROAD AND THE RIVER   *ends.*
HAVE DOORS THAT FACE EACH WAY   TACIT
AND THE ENTRANCE TO THE MOVIE'S
UP AN ALLEY UP THE SIDE.

                                       "Hesitation
PUSHCARTS FOLD AND UNFOLD   *Blues" with*
IN A SUPERMARKET SEA.   *full band*
AND WE BETTER FIND OUT, MAMA,   *up strong*
WHERE IS THE COLORED LAUNDROMAT,   *for a chorus*
SINCE WE MOVED UP TO MOUNT VERNON.   *in the clear*
                                       between verses
RALPH ELLISON AS VESPUCIUS   *then down*
INA–YOURA AT THE MASTHEAD   *under voice*
ARNA BONTEMPS CHIEF CONSULTANT   *softly as*
MOLTO BENE MELLOW BABY PEARLIE MAE   *deep-toned*
SHALOM ALEICHEM JIMMY BALDWIN SAMMY   *distant*
COME WHAT MAY—THE SIGNS POINT: *African*
    GHANA   GUINEA   *drums*
AND THE TOLL BRIDGE FROM WESTCHESTER   *join the*
IS A GANGPLANK ROCKING RISKY   *blues until*
BETWEEN THE DECK AND SHORE   *the music*
OF A BOAT THAT NEVER QUITE   *dies. . . .*
KNEW ITS DESTINATION.

IN THE QUARTER OF THE NEGROES   TACIT
ORNETTE AND CONSTERNATION
CLAIM ATTENTION FROM THE PAPERS
THAT HAVE NO NEWS THAT DAY OF MOSCOW.

IN THE POT BEHIND THE
PAPER DOORS WHAT'S COOKING?
WHAT'S SMELLING, LEONTYNE?   *Delicate*
LIEDER, LOVELY LIEDER   *lieder*
AND A LEAF OF COLLARD GREEN.   *on piano*
LOVELY LIEDER LEONTYNE.   *continues*
    between verses

IN THE SHADOW OF THE NEGROES   *to merge*
    NKRUMAH   *softly*
IN THE SHADOW OF THE NEGROES   *into the*
    NASSER NASSER   *melody of the*
IN THE SHADOW OF THE NEGROES   *"Hesitation*
    ZIK AZIKIWE   *Blues" asking*
CUBA CASTRO GUINEA TOURÉ   *its haunting*
FOR NEED OR PROPAGANDA   *question,*
    KENYATTA   *"How long*
AND THE TOM DOGS OF THE CABIN   *must I*
THE COCOA AND THE CANE BRAKE   *wait?*
THE CHAIN GANG AND THE SLAVE BLOCK   *Can I*
TARRED AND FEATHERED NATIONS   *get it*
SEAGRAM'S AND FOUR ROSES   *now—or*
$5.00 BAGS A DECK OR DAGGA.   *must I*
FILIBUSTER VERSUS VETO   *hesitate?"*
LIKE A SNAPPING TURTLE—   *Suddenly*
WON'T LET GO UNTIL IT THUNDERS   *the drums*
WON'T LET GO UNTIL IT THUNDERS   *roll like*
TEARS THE BODY FROM THE SHADOW   *thunder*
WON'T LET GO UNTIL IT THUNDERS   *as the*
IN THE QUARTER OF THE NEGROES   *music ends*
    sonorously.

AND THEY ASKED ME RIGHT AT CHRISTMAS   TACIT
IF MY BLACKNESS, WOULD I RUB OFF?
I SAID, ASK YOUR MAMA.   *Figure impishly*
into "Dixie"
DREAMS AND NIGHTMARES . . .   *ending in high*
NIGHTMARES . . . DREAMS! OH!   *shrill flute call.*
DREAMING THAT THE NEGROES   TACIT
OF THE SOUTH HAVE TAKEN OVER—
VOTED ALL THE DIXIECRATS
RIGHT OUT OF POWER—
COMES THE *COLORED HOUR:*
MARTIN LUTHER KING IS GOVERNOR OF GEORGIA,
DR. RUFUS CLEMENT HIS CHIEF ADVISOR,
ZELMA WATSON GEORGE THE HIGH GRAND WORTHY.
IN WHITE PILLARED MANSIONS
SITTING ON THEIR WIDE VERANDAS,
WEALTHY NEGROES HAVE WHITE SERVANTS,
WHITE SHARECROPPERS WORK THE BLACK PLANTATIONS,
AND COLORED CHILDREN HAVE WHITE MAMMIES:

     MAMMY FAUBUS
     MAMMY EASTLAND
     MAMMY PATTERSON.
DEAR, *DEAR* DARLING OLD WHITE MAMMIES—
SOMETIMES EVEN BURIED WITH OUR FAMILY!
     DEAR OLD
     MAMMY FAUBUS!
CULTURE, THEY SAY, *IS A TWO-WAY STREET:*

HAND ME MY MINT JULEP, MAMMY.

      MAKE HASTE!

"When the Saints
Go Marching In"
joyously for two
full choruses
with maracas. . . .

Ode to Dinah

IN THE QUARTER OF THE NEGROES   TACIT

WHERE TO SNOW NOW ACCLIMATED

SHADOWS SHOW UP SHARPER,

THE ONE COIN IN THE METER

KEEPS THE GAS ON WHILE THE TV

FAILS TO GET PEARL BAILEY.

SINCE IT'S SNOWING ON THE TV

THIS LAST QUARTER OF CENTENNIAL

100–YEARS EMANCIPATION

MECHANICS NEED REPAIRING

FOR NIAGARA FALLS IS FROZEN

AS IS CUSTOM BELOW ZERO.

MAMA'S FRUITCAKE SENT FROM GEORGIA   *Traditional*

CRUMBLES AS IT'S NIBBLED   *blues*

TO A DISC BY DINAH   *in gospel*

IN THE RUM THAT WAFTS MARACAS   *tempo*

FROM ANOTHER DISTANT QUARTER   *à la Ray*

TO THIS QUARTER OF THE NEGROES   *Charles*

WHERE THE SONG'S MAHALIA'S DAUGHTER   *to fade*

STEP–FATHERED BY BLIND LEMON	*out*
STEP–FATHERED BY	*slowly. . . .*
BLIND LEMON. . . .	

WHEN NIAGARA FALLS IS FROZEN	TACIT
THERE'S A BAR WITH WINDOWS FROSTED	
FROM THE COLD THAT MAKES NIAGARA	
GHOSTLY MONUMENT OF WINTER	
TO A BAND THAT ONCE PASSED OVER	*Verse of*
WITH A WOMAN WITH TWO PISTOLS	*"Battle*
ON A TRAIN THAT LOST NO PASSENGERS	*Hymn*
ON THE LINE WHOSE ROUTE WAS FREEDOM	*of the Republic"*
THROUGH THE JUNGLE OF WHITE DANGER	*through*
TO THE HAVEN OF WHITE QUAKERS	*refrain*
WHOSE HAYMOW WAS A MANGER MANGER	*repeated*
WHERE THE CHRIST CHILD ONCE HAD LAIN.	*ever*
SO THE WHITENESS AND THE WATER	*softer*
MELT TO WATER ONCE AGAIN	*to*
AND THE ROAR OF NIAGARA	*fade*
DROWNS THE RUMBLE OF THAT TRAIN	*out*
DISTANT ALMOST NOW AS DISTANT	*slowly*
AS FORGOTTEN PAIN IN THE QUARTER	*here*
QUARTER OF THE NEGROES	TACIT
WITH A BAR WITH FROSTED WINDOWS	
NO CONDUCTOR AND NO TRAIN.	*Drums*
BONGO–BONGO! CONGO!	*up strong*
BUFFALO AND BONGO!	*for*
NIAGARA OF THE INDIANS!	*interlude*
NIAGARA OF THE CONGO!	*and out.*

BUFFALO TO HARLEM'S OVERNIGHT: TACIT

IN THE QUARTER OF THE NEGROES

WHERE WHITE SHADOWS PASS,

DARK SHADOWS BECOME DARKER BY A SHADE

SUCKED IN BY FAT JUKEBOXES

WHERE DINAH'S SONGS ARE MADE

FROM SLABS OF SILVER SHADOWS.   *"Hesitation*

AS EACH QUARTER CLINKS   *Blues"*

INTO A MILLION POOLS OF QUARTERS   *softly*

TO BE CARTED OFF BY BRINK'S,   *asking*

THE SHADES OF DINAH'S SINGING   *over*

MAKE A SPANGLE OUT OF QUARTERS RINGING   *and*

TO KEEP FAR-OFF CANARIES   *over*

IN SILVER CAGES SINGING.   *its old*

    TELL ME, PRETTY PAPA,   *question,*

    WHAT TIME IS IT NOW?   *"Tell*

    PRETTY PAPA, PRETTY PAPA,   *me*

    WHAT TIME IS IT NOW?   *how*

    DON'T CARE WHAT TIME IT IS—   *long?"*

    GONNA LOVE YOU ANYHOW   *until*

WHILE NIAGARA FALLS IS FROZEN.   *music*

                                                        DIES. . . .

SANTA CLAUS, FORGIVE ME,   TACIT

BUT BABIES BORN IN SHADOWS

IN THE SHADOW OF THE WELFARE

IF BORN PREMATURE

BRING WELFARE CHECKS MUCH SOONER

YET NO PRESENT DOWN THE CHIMNEY.

IN THE SHADOW OF THE WELFARE

CHOCOLATE BABIES BORN IN SHADOWS

ARE TRIBAL NOW NO LONGER
SAVE IN MEMORIES OF GANGRENOUS ICING
ON A TWENTY-STORY HOUSING PROJECT
THE CHOCOLATE GANGRENOUS ICING OF
    JUST WAIT.

TRIBAL NOW NO LONGER PAPA MAMA	*Drums*
IN RELATION TO THE CHILD,	*alone*
ONCE YOUR BROTHER'S KEEPER	*softly*
NOW NOT EVEN KEEPER TO YOUR CHILD—	*merging*
SHELTERED NOW NO LONGER.	*into*
BORN TO GROW UP WILD—	*the*
TRIBAL NOW NO LONGER ONE FOR ALL	*ever-*
AND ALL FOR ONE NO LONGER	*questioning*
EXCEPT IN MEMORIES OF HATE	*"Hesitation*
UMBILICAL IN SULPHUROUS CHOCOLATE:	*Blues"*
GOT TO WAIT—	*beginning*
THIS LAST QUARTER OF CENTENNIAL:	*slowly*
GOT TO WAIT.	*but*
	gradually
I WANT TO GO TO THE SHOW, MAMA.	*building to*
NO SHOW FARE, BABY—	*up-tempo*
NOT THESE DAYS.	*as the*
	metronome
ON THE BIG SCREEN OF THE WELFARE CHECK	*of*
A LYNCHED TOMORROW SWAYS. . . .	*fate*
WITH ALL DELIBERATE SPEED A	*begins*
LYNCHED TOMORROW SWAYS.	*to*
	tick
LIVING 20 YEARS IN 10	*faster*
BETTER HURRY, BETTER HURRY	*and*

BEFORE THE PRESENT BECOMES WHEN   *faster*

    AND YOU'RE 50

    WHEN YOU'RE 40

    40 WHEN YOU'RE 30

    30 WHEN YOU'RE 20   *as the*

    20 WHEN YOU'RE 10   *music*

IN THE QUARTER OF THE NEGROES   *dies*

WHERE THE PENDULUM IS SWINGING

TO THE SHADOW OF THE BLUES,

EVEN WHEN YOU'RE WINNING

THERE'S NO WAY NOT TO LOSE.

WHERE THE SHADOWS MERGE WITH SHADOWS   TACIT

THE DOOR MARKED *LADIES* OPENS INWARD

AND CAN KNOCK THE HADES

OUT OF ONE IN EXIT

IF PUSHED BY HURRIED ENTRANCE.

IN THE SHADOW OF THE QUARTER

WHERE THE PEOPLE ALL ARE DARKER

NOBODY NEED A MARKER.

AMEN IS NOT AN ENDING

BUT JUST A PUNCTUATION.

WHITE FOLKS' RECESSION

IS COLORED FOLKS' DEPRESSION.

THEY ASKED ME RIGHT AT CHRISTMAS,

WOULD I MARRY POCAHONTAS?

MEANWHILE DINAH EATING CHICKEN

NEVER MISSED A BITE

WHEN THE MAN SHOT AT THE WOMAN   *Rim shot.*
AND BY MISTAKE SHOT OUT THE LIGHT.   *Dixieland*
up-tempo
for full chorus
to ending.

Ask Your Mama

FROM THE SHADOWS OF THE QUARTER
SHOUTS ARE WHISPERS CARRYING
TO THE FARTHEREST CORNERS
OF THE NOW KNOWN WORLD:
5TH AND MOUND IN CINCI, 63RD IN CHI,
23RD AND CENTRAL, 18TH STREET AND VINE.
I'VE WRITTEN, CALLED REPEATEDLY,
EVEN RUNG THIS BELL ON SUNDAY, YET
YOUR THIRD-FLOOR TENANT'S NEVER HOME.
DID YOU TELL HER THAT OUR CREDIT OFFICE
HAS NO RECOURSE NOW BUT TO THE LAW?
YES, SIR, I TOLD HER.
WHAT DID SHE SAY?
SAID, TELL YOUR MA.   *Figurine.*

17 SORROWS
AND THE NUMBER
6-0-2.
HIGH BALLS, LOW BALLS:
THE 8-BALL

IS YOU.

7-II!

COME 7

PORGY AND BESS

AT THE PICTURE SHOW.

I NEVER SEEN IT.

BUT I WILL.

YOU KNOW.

IF I HAVE

THE MONEY

TO GO.   *Delicate*

                                                          post-bop

FILLMORE OUT IN FRISCO, 7TH ACROSS THE BAY,   *suggests*

18TH AND VINE IN K.C., 63RD IN CHI,   *pleasant*

ON THE CORNER PICKING SPLINTERS   *evenings and*

OUT OF THE MIDNIGHT SKY   *flirtatious*

IN THE QUARTER OF THE NEGROES   *youth*

AS LEOLA PASSES BY   *as it*

THE MEN CAN ONLY MURMUR   *gradually*

MY! . . . MY! MY!   *weaves*

                                              into its

LUMUMBA LOUIS ARMSTRONG   *pattern*

PATRICE AND PATTI PAGE   *a*

HAMBURGERS PEPSI–COLA   *musical*

KING COLE JUKEBOX PAYOLA   *echo of*

IN THE QUARTER OF THE NEGROES   *Paris*

GOD WILLING DROP A SHILLING   *which*

FORT DE FRANCE, PLACE PIGALLE   *continues*

VINGT FRANCS NICKEL DIME   *until*

BAHIA LAGOS DAKAR LENOX   *very*

KINGSTON TOO GOD WILLING	*softly*
A QUARTER OR A SHILLING. PARIS—	*the*
AT THE DOME VINGT FRANCS WILL DO	*silver*
ROTONDE SELECT DUPONT FLORE	*call*
TALL BLACK STUDENT	*of a*
IN HORN–RIM GLASSES,	*hunting*
WHO AT THE SORBONNE HAS SIX CLASSES,	*horn*
IN THE SHADOW OF THE CLUNY	*is*
CONJURES UNICORN,	*heard*
SPEAKS ENGLISH FRENCH SWAHILI	*far away.*
HAS ALMOST FORGOTTEN MEALIE.	*African*
BUT WHY RIDE ON MULE OR DONKEY	*drums*
WHEN THERE'S A UNICORN?	*begin*
	a softly
NIGHT IN A SÉKOU TOURÉ CAP	*mounting*
DRESSED LIKE A TEDDY BOY	*rumble*
BLOTS COLORS OFF THE MAP.	*soon*
PERHAPS IF IT BE GOD'S WILL	*to fade*
AZIKIWE'S SON, AMEKA	*into a*
SHAKES HANDS WITH EMMETT TILL.	*steady*
BRICKBATS BURST LIKE BUBBLES	*beat*
STONES BURST LIKE BALLOONS	*like*
BUT HEARTS KEEP DOGGED BEATING	*the*
SELDOM BURSTING	*heart*
UNLIKE BUBBLES	
UNLIKE BRICKBATS	TACIT
FAR FROM STONE.	
IN THE QUARTER OF THE NEGROES	
WHERE NO SHADOW WALKS ALONE	
LITTLE MULES AND DONKEYS SHARE	

THEIR GRASS WITH UNICORNS.

Repeat high
flute call
to segue into
up-tempo blues
that continue
behind the
next sequence. . . .

Encounter

I met You on Your way to death,
Though quite by accident
I chose the path I did,
Not knowing there You went.

When I heard the hooting mob
I started to turn back
But, curious, I stood my ground
Directly in its track
And sickened suddenly
At its sound,
Yet did not
Turn back.

So loud the mob cried,
Yet so weak,
Like a sick and muffled sea.
On Your head You had sharp thorns.

You did not look at me—
But on Your back You carried
My own Misery.

Silent One

This little silent one—
He's all the atoms from the sun
And all the grass blades
From the earth
And all the songs
The heart gives birth
To when the throat
Stops singing—
He's my son—
This little
Silent
One.

Junior Addict

The little boy
who sticks a needle in his arm
and seeks an out in other worldly dreams,
who seeks an out in eyes that droop

and ears that close to Harlem screams,
cannot know, of course,
(and has no way to understand)
a sunrise that he cannot see
beginning in some other land—
but destined sure to flood—and soon—
the very room in which he leaves
his needle and his spoon,
the very room in which today the air
is heavy with the drug
of his despair.

      (Yet little can
      tomorrow's sunshine give
      to one who will not live.)

Quick, sunrise, come—
Before the mushroom bomb
Pollutes his stinking air
With better death
Than is his living here,
With viler drugs
Than bring today's release
In poison from the fallout
Of our peace.

      "It's easier to get dope
      than it is to get a job."

Yes, easier to get dope
than to get a job—

daytime or nighttime job,
teen-age, pre-draft,
pre-lifetime job.

Quick, sunrise, come!
Sunrise out of Africa,
Quick, come!
Sunrise, please come!
Come! Come!

Final Call

SEND FOR THE PIED PIPER AND LET HIM PIPE THE RATS AWAY.
SEND FOR ROBIN HOOD TO CLINCH THE ANTI–POVERTY
                               CAMPAIGN.
SEND FOR THE FAIRY QUEEN WITH A WAVE OF THE WAND
TO MAKE US ALL INTO PRINCES AND PRINCESSES.
SEND FOR KING ARTHUR TO BRING THE HOLY GRAIL.
SEND FOR OLD MAN MOSES TO LAY DOWN THE LAW.
SEND FOR JESUS TO PREACH THE SERMON ON THE MOUNT.
SEND FOR DREYFUS TO CRY, *"J'ACCUSE!"*
SEND FOR DEAD BLIND LEMON TO SING THE B FLAT BLUES.
SEND FOR ROBESPIERRE TO SCREAM, *"ÇA IRA! ÇA IRA! ÇA IRA!"*
SEND (GOD FORBID—HE'S NOT DEAD LONG ENOUGH!)
FOR LUMUMBA TO CRY, "FREEDOM NOW!"
SEND FOR LAFAYETTE AND TELL HIM, "HELP! HELP ME!"
SEND FOR DENMARK VESEY CRYING, "FREE!"
FOR CINQUE SAYING, "RUN A NEW FLAG UP THE MAST."

FOR OLD JOHN BROWN WHO KNEW SLAVERY COULDN'T LAST.
SEND FOR LENIN! (DON'T YOU DARE!—HE CAN'T COME HERE!)
SEND FOR TROTSKY! (WHAT? DON'T CONFUSE THE ISSUE, PLEASE!)
SEND FOR UNCLE TOM ON HIS MIGHTY KNEES.
SEND FOR LINCOLN, SEND FOR GRANT.
SEND FOR FREDERICK DOUGLASS, GARRISON, BEECHER, LOWELL.
SEND FOR HARRIET TUBMAN, OLD SOJOURNER TRUTH.
SEND FOR MARCUS GARVEY (WHAT?) SUFI (WHO?) FATHER
                                    DIVINE (WHERE?)
DUBOIS (WHEN?) MALCOLM (OH!) SEND FOR STOKELY. (NO?) THEN
SEND FOR ADAM POWELL ON A NON–SUBPOENA DAY.
SEND FOR THE PIED PIPER TO PIPE OUR RATS AWAY.

    (And if nobody comes, send for me.)

To You

To sit and dream, to sit and read,
To sit and learn about the world
Outside our world of here and now—
    our problem world—
To dream of vast horizons of the soul
Through dreams made whole,
Unfettered free—help me!
All you who are dreamers, too,
Help me make our world anew.
I reach out my hands to you.

Not What Was

By then the poetry is written
and the wild rose of the world
blooms to last so short a time
before its petals fall.
The air is music
and its melody a spiral
until it widens
beyond the tip of time
and so is lost
to poetry and the rose—
belongs instead to vastness beyond form,
to universe that nothing can contain,
to unexplored space
which sends no answers back
to fill the vase unfilled
or spread in lines
upon another page—
that anyhow was never written
because the thought could not escape
the place in which it bloomed
before the rose had gone.

Dinner Guest: Me

I know I am
The Negro Problem
Being wined and dined,
Answering the usual questions
That come to white mind
Which seeks demurely
To probe in polite way
The why and wherewithal
Of darkness U.S.A.—
Wondering how things got this way
In current democratic night,
Murmuring gently
Over *fraises du bois,*
"I'm so ashamed of being white."

The lobster is delicious,
The wine divine,
And center of attention
At the damask table, mine.
To be a Problem on
Park Avenue at eight
Is not so bad.
Solutions to the Problem,
Of course, wait.

Frederick Douglass: 1817–1895

Douglass was someone who,
Had he walked with wary foot
And frightened tread,
From very indecision
Might be dead,
Might have lost his soul,
But instead decided to be bold
And capture every street
On which he set his feet,
To route each path
Toward freedom's goal,
To make each highway
Choose *his* compass' choice,
To all the world cried,
Hear my voice! . . .
Oh, to be a beast, a bird,
Anything but a slave! he said.

Who would be free
Themselves must strike
The first blow, he said.

　　He died in 1895.
　　He is not dead.

Question and Answer

Durban, Birmingham,
Cape Town, Atlanta,
Johannesburg, Watts,
The earth around
Struggling, fighting,
Dying—for what?

A world to gain.

Groping, hoping,
Waiting—for what?

A world to gain.

Dreams kicked asunder,
Why not go under?

There's a world to gain.

But suppose I don't want it,
Why take it?

To remake it.

Crowns and Garlands

Make a garland of Leontynes and Lenas
And hang it about your neck
    Like a lei.
Make a crown of Sammys, Sidneys, Harrys,
Plus Cassius Mohammed Ali Clay.
Put their laurels on your brow
    Today—
Then before you can walk
To the neighborhood corner,
Watch them droop, wilt, fade
    Away.
Though worn in glory on my head,
They do not last a day—
    Not one—
Nor take the place of meat or bread
Or rent that I must pay.
Great names for crowns and garlands!
    Yeah!
I love Ralph Bunche—
But I can't eat him for lunch.

Prime

Uptown on Lenox Avenue
Where a nickel costs a dime,

In these lush and thieving days
When million-dollar thieves
Glorify their million-dollar ways
In the press and on the radio and TV—
　　　But won't let me
　　　Skim even a dime—
I, black, come to my prime
In the section of the niggers
Where a nickel costs a dime.

Black Panther

Pushed into the corner
Of the hobnailed boot,
Pushed into the corner of the
"I-don't-want-to-die" cry,
Pushed into the corner of
"I don't want to study war no more,"
Changed into "Eye for eye,"
The Panther in his desperate boldness
Wears no disguise,
Motivated by the truest
Of the oldest
Lies.

Birmingham Sunday
> (September 15, 1963)

Four little girls
Who went to Sunday School that day
And never came back home at all
But left instead
Their blood upon the wall
With spattered flesh
And bloodied Sunday dresses
Torn to shreds by dynamite
That China made aeons ago—
Did not know
That what China made
Before China was ever Red at all
Would redden with their blood
This Birmingham-on-Sunday wall.

Four tiny girls
Who left their blood upon that wall,
In little graves today await
The dynamite that might ignite
The fuse of centuries of Dragon Kings
Whose tomorrow sings a hymn
The missionaries never taught Chinese
In Christian Sunday School
To implement the Golden Rule.

    Four little girls
Might be awakened someday soon
By songs upon the breeze
As yet unfelt among magnolia trees.

War

The face of war is my face.
The face of war is your face.
    What color
    Is the face
    Of war?
Brown, black, white—
Your face and my face.

Death is the broom
I take in my hands
To sweep the world
    Clean.
I sweep and I sweep
Then mop and I mop.
I dip my broom in blood,
My mop in blood—
And blame you for this,
Because you are *there,*
    Enemy.
It's hard to blame me,

Because I am here—
So I kill you.
And you kill me.
　　My name,
Like your name,
　　Is war.

Un-American Investigators

The committee's fat,
Smug, almost secure
Co-religionists
Shiver with delight
In warm manure
As those investigated—
Too brave to name a name—
Have pseudonyms revealed
In Gentile game
　　Of who,
　　Born Jew,
　　Is who?
Is not your name Lipshitz?
　　Yes.
Did you not change it
For subversive purposes?
　　No.

For nefarious gain?
        Not so.
Are you sure?
The committee shivers
With delight in
Its manure.

CORA UNASHAMED

I

Melton was one of those miserable in-between little places, not large enough to be a town, nor small enough to be a village—that is, a village in the rural, charming sense of the word. Melton had no charm about it. It was merely a nondescript collection of houses and buildings in a region of farms—one of those sad American places with sidewalks, but no paved streets; electric lights, but no sewage; a station, but no trains that stopped, save a jerky local, morning and evening. And it was 150 miles from any city at all—even Sioux City.

Cora Jenkins was one of the least of the citizens of Melton. She was what the people referred to when they wanted to be polite, as a Negress, and when they wanted to be rude, as a nigger—sometimes adding the word "wench" for no good reason, for Cora was usually an inoffensive soul, except that she sometimes cussed.

She had been in Melton for forty years. Born there. Would die there probably. She worked for the Studevants, who treated her like a dog. She stood it. Had to stand it; or work for poorer white folks who would treat her worse; or go jobless. Cora was like a tree—once rooted, she stood, in spite of storms and strife, wind, and rocks, in the earth.

She was the Studevants' maid of all work—washing, ironing, cooking, scrubbing, taking care of kids, nursing old folks, making fires, carrying water.

Cora, bake three cakes for Mary's birthday tomorrow night. You Cora, give Rover a bath in that tar soap I bought. Cora, take Ma some jello, and don't let her have even a taste of that raisin pie. She'll keep us up all night if you do. Cora, iron my stockings. Cora, come here. . . . Cora, put . . . Cora . . . Cora . . . Cora! Cora!

And Cora would answer, "Yes, m'am."

The Studevants thought they owned her, and they were perfectly right: they did. There was something about the teeth in the trap of economic circumstance that kept her in their power practically all her life—in the Studevant kitchen, cooking; in the Studevant parlor, sweeping; in the Studevant backyard, hanging clothes.

You want to know how that could be? How a trap could close so tightly? Here is the outline:

Cora was the oldest of a family of eight children—the Jenkins niggers. The only Negroes in Melton, thank God! Where they came from originally—that is, the old folks— God knows. The kids were born there. The old folks are still there now: Pa drives a junk wagon. The old woman ails around the house, ails and quarrels. Seven kids are gone. Only Cora remains. Cora simply couldn't go, with nobody else to help take care of Ma. And before that she couldn't go, with nobody to see that her brothers and sisters got through school (she the oldest, and Ma ailing). And before that—well, somebody had to help Ma look after one baby behind another that kept on coming.

As a child Cora had no playtime. She always had a little brother, or a little sister in her arms. Bad, crying, bratty babies, hungry and mean. In the eighth grade she quit school and went to work with the Studevants.

After that, she ate better. Half day's work at first, helping Ma at home the rest of the time. Then full days, bringing home her pay to feed her father's children. The old man was rather a drunkard. What little money he made from closet-cleaning, ash-hauling, and junk-dealing he spent mostly on the stuff that makes you forget you have eight kids.

He passed the evenings telling long, comical lies to the white riff-raff of the town, and drinking licker. When his horse died, Cora's money went for a new one to haul her Pa and his rickety wagon around. When the mortgage money came due, Cora's wages kept the man from taking the roof from over their heads. When Pa got in jail, Cora borrowed ten dollars from Mrs. Studevant and got him out.

Cora stinted, and Cora saved, and wore the Studevants' old clothes, and ate the Studevants' leftover food, and brought her pay home. Brothers and sisters grew up. The boys, lonesome, went away, as far as they could from Melton. One by one, the girls left too, mostly in disgrace. "Ruinin' ma name," Pa Jenkins said, "Ruinin' ma good name! They can't go out berryin' but what they come back in disgrace." There was something about the cream-and-tan Jenkins girls that attracted the white farm hands.

Even Cora, the humble, had a lover once. He came to town on a freight train (long ago now), and worked at the livery-stable. (That was before autos got to be so common.)

Everybody said he was an I. W. W. Cora didn't care. He was the first man and the last she ever remembered wanting. She had never known a colored lover. There weren't any around. That was not her fault.

This white boy, Joe, he always smelt like the horses. He was some kind of foreigner. Had an accent, and yellow hair, big hands, and grey eyes.

It was summer. A few blocks beyond the Studevants' house, meadows and orchards and sweet fields stretched away to the far horizon. At night, stars in the velvet sky. Moon sometimes. Crickets and katydids and lightning bugs. The scent of grass. Cora waiting. That boy, Joe, a cigarette spark far off, whistling in the dark. Love didn't take long— Cora with the scent of the Studevants' supper about her, and a cheap perfume. Joe, big and strong and careless as the horses he took care of, smelling like the stable.

Ma would quarrel because Cora came home late, or because none of the kids had written for three or four weeks, or because Pa was drunk again. Thus the summer passed, a dream of big hands and grey eyes.

Cora didn't go anywhere to have her child. Nor tried to hide it. When the baby grew big within her, she didn't feel that it was a disgrace. The Studevants told her to go home and stay there. Joe left town. Pa cussed. Ma cried. One April morning the kid was born. She had grey eyes, and Cora called her Josephine, after Joe.

Cora was humble and shameless before the fact of the child. There were no Negroes in Melton to gossip, and she didn't care what the white people said. They were in another world. Of course, she hadn't expected to marry Joe, or keep him. He was of that other world, too. But the child was hers—a living bridge between two worlds. Let people talk.

Cora went back to work at the Studevants'—coming home at night to nurse her kid, and quarrel with Ma. About that time, Mrs. Art Studevant had a child, too, and Cora nursed it. The Studevants' little girl was named Jessie. As the two children began to walk and talk, Cora sometimes brought Josephine to play with Jessie—until the Studevants objected, saying she could get her work done better if she left her child at home.

"Yes, m'am," said Cora.

But in a little while they didn't need to tell Cora to leave her child at home, for Josephine died of whooping-cough. One rosy afternoon, Cora saw the little body go down into the ground in a white casket that cost four weeks' wages.

Since Ma was ailing, Pa, smelling of licker, stood with her at the grave. The two of them alone. Cora was not humble before the fact of death. As she turned away from the hole, tears came—but at the same time a stream of curses so violent that they made the grave-tenders look up in startled horror.

She cussed out God for taking away the life that she herself had given. She screamed, "My baby! God damn it! My baby! I bear her and you take her away!" She looked at the sky where the sun was setting and yelled in defiance. Pa was amazed and scared. He pulled her up on his rickety wagon and drove off, clattering down the road between green fields and sweet meadows that stretched away to the far horizon. All through the ugly town Cora wept and cursed, using all the bad words she had learned from Pa in his drunkenness.

The next week she went back to the Studevants. She was

gentle and humble in the face of life—she loved their baby. In the afternoons on the back porch, she would pick little Jessie up and rock her to sleep, burying her dark face in the milky smell of the white child's hair.

II

The years passed. Pa and Ma Jenkins only dried up a little. Old Man Studevant died. The old lady had two strokes. Mrs. Art Studevant and her husband began to look their age, greying hair and sagging stomachs. The children were grown, or nearly so. Kenneth took over the management of the hardware store that Grandpa had left. Jack went off to college. Mary was a teacher. Only Jessie remained a child—her last year in high-school. Jessie, nineteen now, and rather slow in her studies, graduating at last. In the Fall she would go to Normal.

Cora hated to think about her going away. In her heart she had adopted Jessie. In that big and careless household it was always Cora who stood like a calm and sheltering tree for Jessie to run to in her troubles. As a child, when Mrs. Art spanked her, as soon as she could, the tears still streaming, Jessie would find her way to the kitchen and Cora. At each school term's end, when Jessie had usually failed in some of her subjects (she quite often failed, being a dull child), it was Cora who saw the report-card first with the bad marks on it. Then Cora would devise some way of breaking the news gently to the old folks.

Her mother was always a little ashamed of stupid Jessie, for Mrs. Art was the civic and social leader of Melton, president of the Woman's Club three years straight, and one of the pillars of her church. Mary, the elder, the teacher, would follow with dignity in her footsteps, but Jessie! That child! Spankings in her youth, and scoldings now, did nothing to Jessie's inner being. She remained a plump, dull, freckled girl, placid and strange. Everybody found fault with her but Cora.

In the kitchen Jessie bloomed. She laughed. She talked. She was sometimes even witty. And she learned to cook wonderfully. With Cora, everything seemed so simple—not hard and involved like algebra, or Latin grammar, or the civic problems of Mama's club, or the sermons at church. Nowhere in Melton, nor with anyone, did Jessie feel so comfortable as with Cora in the kitchen. She knew her mother looked down on her as a stupid girl. And with her father there was no bond. He was always too busy buying and selling to bother with the kids. And often he was off in the city. Old doddering Grandma made Jessie sleepy and sick. Cousin Nora (Mother's cousin) was as stiff and prim as a minister's daughter. And Jessie's older brothers and sister went their ways, seeing Jessie hardly at all, except at the big table at mealtimes.

Like all the unpleasant things in the house, Jessie was left to Cora. And Cora was happy. To have a child to raise, a child the same age as her Josephine would have been, gave her a purpose in life, a warmth inside herself. It was Cora who nursed and mothered and petted and loved the dull little Jessie through the years. And now Jessie was a young woman, graduating (late) from high-school.

But something had happened to Jessie. Cora knew it before Mrs. Art did. Jessie was not too stupid to have a boyfriend. She told Cora about it like a mother. She was afraid to tell Mrs. Art. Afraid! Afraid! Afraid!

Cora said, "I'll tell her." So, humble and unashamed about life, one afternoon she marched into Mrs. Art's sun-porch and announced quite simply, "Jessie's going to have a baby."

Cora smiled, but Mrs. Art stiffened like a bolt. Her mouth went dry. She rose like a soldier. Sat down. Rose again. Walked straight toward the door, turned around, and whispered, "What?"

"Yes, m'am, a baby. She told me. A little child. Its father is Willie Matsoulos, whose folks runs the ice-cream stand on Main. She told me. They want to get married, but Willie ain't here now. He don't know yet about the child."

Cora would have gone on humbly and shamelessly talking about the little unborn had not Mrs. Art fallen into uncontrollable hysterics. Cousin Nora came running from the library, her glasses on a chain. Old Lady Studevant's wheel-chair rolled up, doddering and shaking with excitement. Jessie came, when called, red and sweating, but had to go out, for when her mother looked up from the couch and saw her she yelled louder than ever. There was a rush for camphor bottles and water and ice. Crying and praying followed all over the house. Scandalization! Oh, my Lord! Jessie was in trouble.

"She ain't in trouble neither," Cora insisted. "No trouble having a baby you want. I had one."

"Shut up, Cora!"

"Yes, m'am. . . . But I had one."

"Hush, I tell you."

"Yes, m'am."

|||

Then it was that Cora began to be shut out. Jessie was confined to her room. That afternoon, when Miss Mary came home from school, the four white women got together behind closed doors in Mrs. Art's bedroom. For once Cora cooked supper in the kitchen without being bothered by an interfering voice. Mr. Studevant was away in Des Moines. Somehow Cora wished he was home. Big and gruff as he was, he had more sense than the women. He'd probably make a shot-gun wedding out of it. But left to Mrs. Art, Jessie would never marry the Greek boy at all. This Cora knew. No man had been found yet good enough for sister Mary to mate with. Mrs. Art had ambitions which didn't include the likes of Greek ice-cream makers' sons.

Jessie was crying when Cora brought her supper up. The black woman sat down on the bed and lifted the white girl's head in her dark hands. "Don't you mind, honey," Cora said. "Just sit tight, and when the boy comes back I'll tell him how things are. If he loves you he'll want you. And there ain't no reason why you can't marry, neither—you both white. Even if he is a foreigner, he's a right nice boy."

"He loves me," Jessie said. "I know he does. He said so."

But before the boy came back (or Mr. Studevant either) Mrs. Art and Jessie went to Kansas City. "For an Easter shopping trip," the weekly paper said.

Then Spring came in full bloom, and the fields and orchards at the edge of Melton stretched green and beautiful to the far horizon. Cora remembered her own Spring, twenty years ago, and a great sympathy and pain welled up in her heart for Jessie, who was the same age that Josephine would have been, had she lived. Sitting on the kitchen porch shelling peas, Cora thought back over her own life—years and years of working for the Studevants; years and years of going home to nobody but Ma and Pa; little Josephine dead; only Jessie to keep her heart warm. And she knew that Jessie was the dearest thing she had in the world. All the time the girl was gone now, she worried.

After ten days, Mrs. Art and her daughter came back. But Jessie was thinner and paler than she'd ever been in her life. There was no light in her eyes at all. Mrs. Art looked a little scared as they got off the train.

"She had an awful attack of indigestion in Kansas City," she told the neighbors and club women. "That's why I stayed away so long, waiting for her to be able to travel. Poor Jessie! She looks healthy, but she's never been a strong child. She's one of the worries of my life." Mrs. Art talked a lot, explained a lot, about how Jessie had eaten the wrong things in Kansas City.

At home, Jessie went to bed. She wouldn't eat. When Cora brought her food up, she whispered, "The baby's gone."

Cora's face went dark. She bit her lips to keep from cursing. She put her arms about Jessie's neck. The girl cried. Her food went untouched.

A week passed. They tried to *make* Jessie eat then. But the food wouldn't stay on her stomach. Her eyes grew yellow, her tongue white, her heart acted crazy. They called in old Doctor Brown, but within a month (as quick as that) Jessie died.

She never saw the Greek boy any more. Indeed, his father had lost his license, "due to several complaints by the mothers of children, backed by the Woman's Club," that he was selling tainted ice cream. Mrs. Art Studevant had started a campaign to rid the town of objectionable tradespeople and questionable characters. Greeks were bound to be one or the other. For a while they even closed up Pa Jenkins' favorite bootlegger. Mrs. Studevant thought this would please Cora, but Cora only said, "Pa's been drinkin' so long he just as well keep on." She refused further to remark on her employer's campaign of purity. In the midst of this clean-up Jessie died.

On the day of the funeral, the house was stacked with flowers. (They held the funeral, not at the church, but at home, on account of old Grandma Studevant's infirmities.) All the family dressed in deep mourning. Mrs. Art was prostrate. As the hour for the services approached, she revived, however, and ate an omelette, "to help me go through the afternoon."

"And Cora," she said, "cook me a little piece of ham with it. I feel so weak."

"Yes, m'am."

The senior class from the high-school came in a body. The Woman's Club came with their badges. The Reverend Doctor McElroy had on his highest collar and longest coat. The choir sat behind the coffin, with a special soloist to sing "He Feedeth His Flocks Like a Shepherd." It was a beautiful Spring afternoon, and a beautiful funeral.

Except that Cora was there. Of course, her presence created no comment (she was the family servant), but it was what she did, and how she did it, that has remained the talk of Melton to this day—for Cora was not humble in the face of death.

When the Reverend Doctor McElroy had finished his eulogy, and the senior class had read their memorials, and the songs had been sung, and they were about to allow the relatives and friends to pass around for one last look at Jessie Studevant, Cora got up from her seat by the dining-room door. She said, "Honey, I want to say something." She spoke as if she were addressing Jessie. She approached the coffin and held out her brown hands over the white girl's body. Her face moved in agitation. People sat stone-still and there was a long pause. Suddenly she screamed. "They killed you! And for nothin'. . . . They killed your child. . . . They took you away from here in the Springtime of your life, and now you'se gone, gone, gone!"

Folks were paralyzed in their seats.

Cora went on: "They preaches you a pretty sermon and they don't say nothin'. They sings you a song, and they don't say nothin'. But Cora's here, honey, and she's gone tell 'em what they done to you. She's gonna tell 'em why they took you to Kansas City."

A loud scream rent the air. Mrs. Art fell back in her chair, stiff as a board. Cousin Nora and sister Mary sat like stones. The men of the family rushed forward to grab Cora. They stumbled over wreaths and garlands. Before they could reach her, Cora pointed her long fingers at the women in black and said, "They killed you, honey. They killed you and your child. I told 'em you loved it, but they didn't care. They killed it before it was . . ."

A strong hand went around Cora's waist. Another grabbed her arm. The Studevant males half pulled, half pushed her through the aisles of folding chairs, through the crowded dining-room, out into the empty kitchen, through the screen door into the backyard. She struggled against them all the way, accusing their women. At the door she sobbed, great tears coming for the love of Jessie.

She sat down on a wash-bench in the backyard, crying. In the parlor she could hear the choir singing weakly. In a few moments she gathered herself together, and went back into the house. Slowly, she picked up her few belongings from the kitchen and pantry, her aprons and her umbrella, and went off down the alley, home to Ma. Cora never came back to work for the Studevants.

Now she and Ma live from the little garden they raise, and from the junk Pa collects—when they can take by main force a part of his meager earnings before he buys his licker.

Anyhow, on the edge of Melton, the Jenkins niggers, Pa and Ma and Cora, somehow manage to get along.

HOME

When the boy came back, there were bright stickers and tags in strange languages the home folks couldn't read all over his bags, and on his violin case. They were the marks of custom stations at far-away borders, big hotels in European cities, and steamers that crossed the ocean a long way from Hopkinsville. They made the leather-covered bags and black violin case look very gay and circus-like. They made white people on the train wonder about the brown-skinned young man to whom the baggage belonged. And when he got off at a village station in Missouri, the loafers gathered around in a crowd, staring.

Roy Williams had come home from abroad to visit his folks, his mother and sister and brothers who still remained in the old home town. Roy had been away seven or eight years, wandering the world. He came back very well dressed, but awfully thin. He wasn't well.

It was this illness that had made Roy come home, really. He had a feeling that he was going to die, and he wanted to see his mother again. This feeling about death had been coming over him gradually for two or three years now. It seemed to him that it must have started in Vienna, that gay but dying city in Central Europe where so many people were hungry, and yet some still had money to buy champagne and caviar and women in the night-clubs where Roy's orchestra played.

But the glittering curtains of Roy's jazz were lined with death. It made him sick to see people fainting in the streets of Vienna from hunger, while others stuffed themselves with wine and food. And it made him sad to refuse the young white women trailing behind him when he came home from work late at night, offering their bodies for a little money to buy something to eat.

In Vienna Roy had a room to himself because he wanted to study and keep up his music. He studied under one of the best violin teachers. But it was hard to keep beautiful and hungry women out of his place, who wanted to give themselves to a man who had a job because in turn the man might let them sleep in his room, or toss them a few bills to take home to their starving parents.

"Folks catch hell in Europe," Roy thought. "I never saw people as hungry as this, not even Negroes at home."

But it was even worse when the orchestra moved back to Berlin. Behind the apparent solidity of that great city, behind doors where tourists never passed, hunger and pain were beyond understanding. And the police were beating people who protested, or stole, or begged. Yet in the cabaret where Roy played, crowds of folks still spent good gold. They laughed and danced every night and didn't give a damn about the children sleeping in doorways outside, or the men who built houses of packing boxes, or the women who walked the streets to pick up trade.

It was in Berlin that the sadness weighed most heavily on Roy. And it was there that he began to cough. One night in Prague, he had a hemorrhage. When he got to Paris, his girl-friend took care of him, and he got better. But he had all the time, from then on, that feeling that he was going to die. The cough stayed, and the sadness. So he came home to see his mother.

He landed in New York on the day that Hoover drove the veterans out of Washington. He stayed a couple of days in Harlem. Most of his old friends there, musicians and actors, were hungry and out of work. When they saw Roy dressed so well, they asked him for money. And at night women whispered in the streets, "Come here, baby! I want to see you, darlin'."

"Rotten everywhere," Roy thought. "I want to go home."

That last night in Harlem, he couldn't sleep. He thought of his mother. In the morning he sent her a telegram that he was on his way.

II

"An uppity nigger," said the white loafers when they saw him standing, slim and elegant, on the station platform in the September sunlight, surrounded by his bags with the bright stickers. Roy had got off a Pullman—something unusual for a Negro in those parts.

"God damn!" said the white loafers.

Suddenly a nasal voice broke out, "Well, I'll be dogged if it ain't Roy Williams!"

Roy recognized an old playmate, Charlie Mumford, from across the alley—a tall red-necked white boy in overalls. He took off his glove and held out his hand. The white man took it, but he didn't shake it long. Roy had forgotten he wasn't in Europe, wearing gloves and shaking hands glibly with a white man! Damn!

"Where you been, boy?" the white fellow asked.

"Paris," said Roy.

"What'd yuh come back for?" a half-southern voice drawled from the edge of a baggage truck.

"I wanted to come home," said Roy, "to see my mother."

"I hope she's gladder to see yuh than we are," another white voice drawled.

Roy picked up his bags, since there were no porters, and carried them toward a rusty old Ford that seemed to be a taxi. He felt dizzy and weak. The smoke and dust of travel had made him cough a lot. The eyes of the white men about the station were not kind. He heard some one mutter, "Nigger." His skin burned. For the first time in half a dozen years he felt his color. He was home.

|||

Sing a song of Dixie, cotton bursting in the sun, shade of chinaberry trees, persimmons after frost has fallen. Hounds treeing possums October nights. O, sweet potatoes, hot, with butter in their yellow hearts.

"Son, I'm glad you's done come home. What can Ma

cook for you? I know you's hungry for some real food. Corn bread and greens and salt pork. Lawd! . . . You's got some mighty nice clothes, honey, but you looks right thin. . . . Chile, I hope you's gonna stay home awhile. . . . These colored girls here'll go crazy about you. They fightin' over you already. . . . Honey, when you plays that violin o' your'n it makes me right weak, it's so purty. . . . Play yo' violin, boy! God's done give you a gift! Yes, indeedy! . . . It's funny how all these Hopkinsville white folks is heard about you already. De woman where yo' sister works say she read someplace 'bout that orchestry you was playin' with in Paris. She says fo' Sister to bring you up to de house to play fo' her sometime. I told Sister, no indeedy, you don't go around playin' at nobody's house. Told her to tell that white woman de Deacon's Board's arrangin' a concert at de church fo' you where everybody can come and pay twenty-five cents to de glory of God and hear you play. Ain't that right, son? You gwine play fo' de Lawd here in Hopkinsville. You been playin' fo' de devil every night all over Europy. . . . Jesus have mercy! Lemme go and get ma washin' out! And whiles you's practicin', I'm gonna make you a pumpkin pie this afternoon. I can see yo' mouth a-waterin' now. . . . Honey, Ma's sho glad you's done come home. . . . Play yo' violin, son!"

IV

CAPRICE VIENNOIS
AIR FOR G STRING
SONATA IN A
AVE MARIA
THE GYPSY DANCES

What little house anywhere was ever big enough to hold Brahms and Beethoven, Bach and César Franck? Certainly not Sister Sarah Williams's house in Hopkinsville. When Roy played, ill as he was, the notes went bursting out the windows and the colored folks and white folks in the street heard them. The classic Mr. Brahms coming out of a nigger's house in the southern end of Missouri. O, my God! Play yo' violin, Roy! Tonight's your concert.

The Deacons and the Ladies' Aid sold a lot of tickets to the white folks they worked for. Roy's home-coming concert at Shiloh Church was a financial success. The front rows were fifty cents and filled with white folks. The rest of the seats were a quarter and filled with Negroes. Methodist and Baptist both came, forgetting churchly rivalry. And there were lots of colored girls with powdered bonbon faces—sweet black and brown and yellow girls with red mouths pointed at Roy. There was lots of bustle and perfume and smothered giggling and whispered talk as the drab little church filled. New shoes screeched up and down the aisles. People applauded because it was past the hour, but the concert started colored folks' time anyhow—late. The church was crowded.

V

Hello, Mr. Brahms on a violin from Vienna at a colored church in Hopkinsville, Missouri. The slender brown-skin hands of a sick young man making you sing for an audience of poor white folks and even poorer Negroes. Good-evenin', Mr. Brahms, a long ways from home, travellin' in answer to your dream, singin' across the world. I had a dream, too, Mr. Brahms, a big dream that can't come true, now. Dream of a great stage in a huge hall, like Carnegie Hall or the Salle Gaveau. And you, Mr. Brahms, singin' out into the darkness, singin' so strong and true that a thousand people look up at me like they do at Roland Hayes singing the Crucifixion. Jesus, I dreamed like that once before I got sick and had to come home.

And here I am giving my first concert in America for my mother and the Deacons of Shiloh Church and the quarters and fifty cent pieces they've collected from Brahms and me for the glory of God. This ain't Carnegie Hall. I've only just come home. . . . But they're looking at me. They're all looking at me. The white folks in the front rows and the Negroes in the back. Like one pair of eyes looking at me.

This, my friends . . . I should say, *Ladies and Gentlemen.* (There are white folks in the audience who are not my friends.) . . . This is the *Meditation from Thaïs* by Massenet. . . . This is the broken heart of a dream come true not true. This is music, and me, sitting on the door-step of the world needing you. . . . O, body of life and love with black hands and brown limbs and white breasts and a golden face with lips like a violin bowed for singing. . . . Steady, Roy! It's hot in this crowded church, and you're sick as hell. . . . This, the dream and the dreamer, wandering in the desert from Hopkinsville to Vienna in love with a street-walker named Music. . . . Listen, you bitch, I want you to be beautiful as the moon in the night on the edge of the Missouri hills. I'll make you beautiful. . . . The *Meditation from Thaïs*. . . . You remember, Ma (even to hear me play, you've got your seat in the amen corner tonight like on Sunday mornings when you come to talk to God), you remember that Kreisler record we had on the phonograph with the big horn when I was a kid? Nobody liked it but me, but you didn't care how many times I played it, over and over. . . . Where'd you get my violin? Half the time you didn't have the money to pay old man Miller for my lesson every week. . . . God rest his unpaid soul, as the Catholics say. . . . Why did you cry, Ma, when I went away with the minstrel show, playing coon songs through the South instead of hymns? What did you cry for, Ma, when I wrote you I had a job with a night-club jazz band on State Street in Chicago? . . . Why did you pray all night when I told you we had a contract to go to Berlin and work in a cabaret there? I tried to explain to you that the best violin teachers in the world were in Berlin and that I'd come back playing like that Kreisler record on the old victrola. . . . And didn't I send you money home? . . . Spray like sand in the eyes. . . . O, dream on the door-step of the world! Thaïs! Thaïs! . . . You sure don't look like Thaïs, you scrawny white woman in a cheap coat and red hat staring up at me from the first row. You don't look a bit like Thaïs. What is it you want the music to give you? What do you want from me? . . . This is Hopkinsville, Missouri. . . . Look at all those brown girls back there in the crowd of Negroes, leaning toward me and the music. First time most of them ever saw a man in evening clothes, black or white. First time most of them ever heard the *Meditation from Thaïs*. First time they ever had one of their own race come home from abroad playing a violin. See them looking proud at me and music over the heads of the white folks in the first rows, over the head of the white woman in the cheap coat and red hat who knows what music's all about. . . . Who are you, lady?

When the concert was over, even some of the white folks shook Roy's hand and said it was wonderful. The colored folks said, "Boy, you sure can play!" Roy was shaking a little and his eyes burned and he wanted terribly to cough. Pain shot across his shoulders. But he smiled his concert-jazz-band smile that the gold spending ladies of the European night-clubs had liked so much. And he held out a feverish hand to everybody. The white woman in the red hat waited at the edge of the crowd.

When people thinned out a little from the pulpit, she came to Roy and shook his hand. She spoke of symphony concerts in St. Louis, of the fact that she was a teacher of music, of piano and violin, but that she had no pupils like Roy, that never in the town of Hopkinsville had anyone else played so beautifully. Roy looked into her thin, freckled face and was glad she knew what it was all about. He was glad she liked music.

"That's Miss Reese," his mother told him after she had gone. "An old maid musicianer at the white high school."

"Yes'm," said Roy. "She understands music."

VI

The next time he saw Miss Reese was at the white high school shortly after it opened the fall session. One morning a note had come asking him if he would play for her Senior class in music appreciation some day. She would accompany him if he would bring his music. It seems that one of Miss Reese's duties was the raising of musical standards in Hopkinsville; she had been telling her students about Bach and Mozart, and she would so appreciate it if Roy would visit the school and play those two great masters for her young people. She wrote him a nice note on clean white paper.

Roy went. His mother thought it was a great honor for the white high school to send for her colored son to play for them. "That Miss Reese's a right nice woman," Sister Williams said to her boy. "Sendin' for you to play up there at de school. First time I ever knowed 'em to have a Negro in there for anything but cleanin' up, and I been in Hopkinsville a long time. Go and play for 'em, son, to de glory of God!"

Roy played. But it was one of those days when his throat was hot and dry, and his eyes burned. He had been coughing all morning and, as he played, his breath left him and he stood covered with a damp sweat. He played badly.

But Miss Reese was more than kind to him. She accompanied him at the piano. And when he had finished, she turned to the assembled class of white kids sprawled in their seats and said, "This is art, my dear young people, this is true art!"

The students went home that afternoon and told their parents that a dressed-up nigger had come to school with a

violin and played a lot of funny pieces nobody but Miss
Reese liked. They went on to say that Miss Reese had
grinned all over herself and cried, "Wonderful!" And had
even bowed to the nigger when he went out!

Roy went home to bed. He was up and down these days,
thinner and thinner all the time, weaker and weaker. Some-
times not practicing any more. Often not eating the food
his mother cooked for him, or that his sister brought from
where she worked. Sometimes being restless and hot in the
night and getting up and dressing, even to spats and yellow
gloves, and walking the streets of the little town at ten and
eleven o'clock after nearly every one else had gone to bed.
Midnight was late in Hopkinsville. But for years Roy had
worked at night. It was hard for him to sleep before morning
now.

But one night he walked out of the house for the last
time. The moon had risen and Roy scarcely needed to light
the oil lamp to dress by when he got up. The moon shone
into his little room, across the white counterpane of his bed,
down onto the bags with the bright stickers piled against the
wall. It glistened on the array of medicine bottles on the side
table. But Roy lighted the light, the better to see himself in
the warped mirror of the dresser. Ashy pale his face was, that
had once been brown. His cheeks were sunken. Trembling,
he put on his suit and spats and his yellow gloves and soft felt
hat. He got into an overcoat. He took a cane that he carried
lately from weakness rather than from style. And he went
out into the autumn moonlight.

Tiptoeing through the parlor, he heard his mother snor-
ing on the couch there. (She had given up her room to
him.) The front door was still unlocked. His brothers, Roy

thought, were out with their girlfriends. His sister had gone to bed.

In the streets it was very quiet. Misty with moonlight, the trees stood half clad in autumn leaves. Roy walked under the dry falling leaves toward the center of the town, breathing in the moonlight air and swinging his cane. Night and the streets always made him feel better. He remembered the boulevards of Paris and the Unter den Linden. He remembered Tauber singing *Wien, Du Stadt Meiner Traume.* His mind went back to the lights and the music of the cities of Europe. How like a dream that he had ever been in Europe at all, he thought. Ma never had any money. Her kids had barely managed to get through the grade school. There was no higher school for Negroes in Hopkinsville. For him there had been only a minstrel show to run away with for further education. Then that chance with a jazz band going to Berlin. And his violin for a mistress all the time—with the best teachers his earnings could pay for abroad. Jazz at night and the classics in the morning. Hard work and hard practice, until his violin sang like nobody's business. Music, real music! Then he began to cough in Berlin.

Roy was passing lots of people now in the brightness of the main street, but he saw none of them. He saw only dreams and memories, and heard music. Some of the people stopped to stare and grin at the flare of the European coat on his slender brown body. Spats and a cane on a young nigger in Hopkinsville, Missouri! What's the big idea, heh? A little white boy or two catcalled, "Hey, coon!" But everything might have been all right, folks might only have laughed or commented or cussed, had not a rather faded woman in a cheap coat and a red hat, a white woman, stepping out of the drug store just as Roy passed, bowed pleasantly to him, "Good evening."

Roy started, bowed, nodded, "Good evening, Miss Reese," and was glad to see her. Forgetting he wasn't in Europe, he took off his hat and his gloves, and held out his hand to this lady who understood music. They smiled at each other, the sick young colored man and the aging music teacher in the light of the main street. Then she asked him if he was still working on the Sarasate.

"Yes," Roy said. "It's lovely."

"And have you heard that marvellous Heifetz record of it?" Miss Reese inquired.

Roy opened his mouth to reply when he saw the woman's face suddenly grow pale with horror. Before he could turn around to learn what her eyes had seen, he felt a fist like a ton of bricks strike his jaw. There was a flash of lightning in his brain as his head hit the edge of the plate glass window of the drug store. Miss Reese screamed. The sidewalk filled with white young ruffians with red-necks, open sweaters, and fists doubled up to strike. The movies had just let out and the crowd, passing by and seeing, objected to a Negro talking to a white woman—insulting a White Woman—attacking a WHITE woman—RAPING A WHITE WOMAN. They saw Roy remove his gloves and bow. When Miss Reese screamed after Roy had been struck, they were sure he had been making love to her. And before the story got beyond the rim of the crowd, Roy had been trying to rape her, right there on the main street in front of the brightly-lighted windows of the drug store. Yes, he did, too! Yes, sir!

So they knocked Roy down. They trampled on his hat

and cane and gloves as a dozen men tried to get to him to pick him up—so some one else could have the pleasure of knocking him down again. They struggled over the privilege of knocking him down.

Roy looked up from the sidewalk at the white mob around him. His mouth was full of blood and his eyes burned. His clothes were dirty. He wondered why Miss Reese had stopped to ask him about Sarasate. He knew he would never get home to his mother now.

Some one jerked him to his feet. Some one spat in his face. (It looked like his old playmate, Charlie Mumford.) Somebody cussed him for being a nigger, and another kicked him from behind. And all the men and boys in the lighted street began to yell and scream like mad people, and to snarl like dogs, and to pull at the little Negro in spats they were dragging through the town towards the woods.

The little Negro whose name was Roy Williams began to choke on the blood in his mouth. And the roar of their voices and the scuff of their feet were split by the moonlight into a thousand notes like a Beethoven sonata. And when the white folks left his brown body, stark naked, strung from a tree at the edge of town, it hung there all night, like a violin for the wind to play.

THE BLUES I'M PLAYING

I

Oceola Jones, pianist, studied under Philippe in Paris. Mrs. Dora Ellsworth paid her bills. The bills included a little apartment on the Left Bank and a grand piano. Twice a year Mrs. Ellsworth came over from New York and spent part of her time with Oceola in the little apartment. The rest of her time abroad she usually spent at Biarritz or Juan les Pins, where she would see the new canvases of Antonio Bas, a young Spanish painter who also enjoyed the patronage of Mrs. Ellsworth. Bas and Oceola, the woman thought, both had genius. And whether they had genius or not, she loved them, and took good care of them.

Poor dear lady, she had no children of her own. Her husband was dead. And she had no interest in life now save art, and the young people who created art. She was very rich, and it gave her pleasure to share her richness with beauty. Except that she was sometimes confused as to where beauty lay—in the youngsters or in what they made, in the creators or the creation. Mrs. Ellsworth had been known to help charming young people who wrote terrible poems, blue-eyed young men who painted awful pictures. And she once turned down a garlic-smelling soprano-singing girl who, a few years later, had all the critics in New York at her feet. The girl was so sallow. And she really needed a bath, or at least a mouth wash, on the day when Mrs. Ellsworth went to hear her sing at an East Side settlement house. Mrs. Ellsworth had sent a small check and let it go at that—since, however, living to regret bitterly her lack of musical acumen in the face of garlic.

About Oceola, though, there had been no doubt. The Negro girl had been highly recommended to her by Ormond Hunter, the music critic, who often went to Harlem to hear the church concerts there, and had thus listened twice to Oceola's playing.

"A most amazing tone," he had told Mrs. Ellsworth, knowing her interest in the young and unusual. "A flair for the piano such as I have seldom encountered. All she needs is training—finish, polish, a repertoire."

"Where is she?" asked Mrs. Ellsworth at once. "I will hear her play."

By the hardest, Oceola was found. By the hardest, an appointment was made for her to come to East 63rd Street and play for Mrs. Ellsworth. Oceola had said she was busy every day. It seemed that she had pupils, rehearsed a church choir, and played almost nightly for colored house parties or dances. She made quite a good deal of money. She wasn't tremendously interested, it seemed, in going way downtown to play for some elderly lady she had never heard of, even if the request did come from the white critic, Ormond Hunter, via the pastor of the church whose choir she rehearsed, and to which Mr. Hunter's maid belonged.

It was finally arranged, however. And one afternoon, promptly on time, black Miss Oceola Jones rang the door bell of white Mrs. Dora Ellsworth's grey stone house just off Madison. A butler who actually wore brass buttons opened the door, and she was shown upstairs to the music room. (The butler had been warned of her coming.) Ormond Hunter was already there, and they shook hands. In a moment, Mrs. Ellsworth came in, a tall stately grey-haired lady in black with a scarf that sort of floated behind her. She was tremendously intrigued at meeting Oceola, never having had before amongst all her artists a black one. And she was greatly impressed that Ormond Hunter should have recommended the girl. She began right away, treating her as a protegee; that is, she began asking her a great many questions she would not dare ask anyone else at first meeting, except a protegee. She asked her how old she was and where her mother and father were and how she made her living and whose music she liked best to play and was she married and would she take one lump or two in her tea, with lemon or cream?

After tea, Oceola played. She played the Rachmaninoff *Prelude in C Sharp Minor.* She played from the Liszt *Études.* She played the *St. Louis Blues.* She played Ravel's *Pavane pour une Infante Défunte.* And then she said she had to go. She was playing that night for a dance in Brooklyn for the benefit of the Urban League.

Mrs. Ellsworth and Ormond Hunter breathed, "How lovely!"

Mrs. Ellsworth said, "I am quite overcome, my dear. You play so beautifully." She went on further to say, "You must let me help you. Who is your teacher?"

"I have none now," Oceola replied. "I teach pupils

myself. Don't have time any more to study—nor money either."

"But you must have time," said Mrs. Ellsworth, "and money, also. Come back to see me on Tuesday. We will arrange it, my dear."

And when the girl had gone, she turned to Ormond Hunter for advice on piano teachers to instruct those who already had genius, and need only to be developed.

II

Then began one of the most interesting periods in Mrs. Ellsworth's whole experience in aiding the arts. The period of Oceola. For the Negro girl, as time went on, began to occupy a greater and greater place in Mrs. Ellsworth's interests, to take up more and more of her time, and to use up more and more of her money. Not that Oceola ever asked for money, but Mrs. Ellsworth herself seemed to keep thinking of so much more Oceola needed.

At first it was hard to get Oceola to need anything. Mrs. Ellsworth had the feeling that the girl mistrusted her generosity, and Oceola did—for she had never met anybody interested in pure art before. Just to be given things for *art's sake* seemed suspicious to Oceola.

That first Tuesday, when the colored girl came back at Mrs. Ellsworth's request, she answered the white woman's questions with a why-look in her eyes.

"Don't think I'm being personal, dear," said Mrs. Ellsworth, "but I must know your background in order to help you. Now, tell me . . ."

Oceola wondered why on earth the woman wanted to help her. However, since Mrs. Ellsworth seemed interested in her life's history, she brought it forth so as not to hinder the progress of the afternoon, for she wanted to get back to Harlem by six o'clock.

Born in Mobile in 1903. Yes, m'am, she was older than she looked. Papa had a band, that is her step-father. Used to play for all the lodge turn-outs, picnics, dances, barbecues. You could get the best roast pig in the world in Mobile. Her mother used to play the organ in church, and when the deacons bought a piano after the big revival, her mama played that, too. Oceola played by ear for a long while until her mother taught her notes. Oceola played an organ, also, and a cornet.

"My, my," said Mrs. Ellsworth.

"Yes, m'am," said Oceola. She had played and practiced on lots of instruments in the South before her step-father died. She always went to band rehearsals with him.

"And where was your father, dear?" asked Mrs. Ellsworth.

"My step-father had the band," replied Oceola. Her mother left off playing in the church to go with him traveling in Billy Kersands' Minstrels. He had the biggest mouth in the world, Kersands did, and used to let Oceola put both her hands in it at a time and stretch it. Well, she and her mama and step-papa settled down in Houston. Sometimes her parents had jobs and sometimes they didn't. Often they were hungry, but Oceola went to school and had a regular piano-teacher, an old German woman, who gave her what technique she had today.

"A fine old teacher," said Oceola. "She used to teach me half the time for nothing. God bless her."

"Yes," said Mrs. Ellsworth. "She gave you an excellent foundation."

"Sure did. But my step-papa died, got cut, and after that Mama didn't have no more use for Houston so we moved to St. Louis. Mama got a job playing for the movies in a Market Street theater, and I played for a church choir, and saved some money and went to Wilberforce. Studied piano there, too. Played for all the college dances. Graduated. Came to New York and heard Rachmaninoff and was crazy about him. Then Mama died, so I'm keeping the little flat myself. One room is rented out."

"Is she nice," asked Mrs. Ellsworth, "your roomer?"

"It's not a she," said Oceola. "He's a man. I hate women roomers."

"Oh!" said Mrs. Ellsworth. "I should think all roomers would be terrible."

"He's right nice," said Oceola. "Name's Pete Williams."

"What does he do?" asked Mrs. Ellsworth.

"A Pullman porter," replied Oceola, "but he's saving money to go to Med school. He's a smart fellow."

But it turned out later that he wasn't paying Oceola any rent.

That afternoon, when Mrs. Ellsworth announced that she had made her an appointment with one of the best piano teachers in New York, the black girl seemed pleased. She recognized the name. But how, she wondered, would she find time for study, with her pupils and her choir, and all. When Mrs. Ellsworth said that she would cover her *entire* living expenses, Oceola's eyes were full of that why-look, as though she didn't believe it.

"I have faith in your art, dear," said Mrs. Ellsworth, at

parting. But to prove it quickly, she sat down that very evening and sent Oceola the first monthly check so that she would no longer have to take in pupils or drill choirs or play at house parties. And so Oceola would have faith in art, too.

That night Mrs. Ellsworth called up Ormond Hunter and told him what she had done. And she asked if Mr. Hunter's maid knew Oceola, and if she supposed that that man rooming with her were anything to her. Ormond Hunter said he would inquire.

Before going to bed, Mrs. Ellsworth told her housekeeper to order a book called "Nigger Heaven" on the morrow, and also anything else Brentano's had about Harlem. She made a mental note that she must go up there sometime, for she had never yet seen that dark section of New York; and now that she had a Negro protegee, she really ought to know something about it. Mrs. Ellsworth couldn't recall ever having known a single Negro before in her whole life, so she found Oceola fascinating. And just as black as she herself was white.

Mrs. Ellsworth began to think in bed about what gowns would look best on Oceola. Her protegee would have to be well-dressed. She wondered, too, what sort of a place the girl lived in. And who that man was who lived with her. She began to think that really Oceola ought to have a place to herself. It didn't seem quite respectable. . . .

When she woke up in the morning, she called her car and went by her dressmaker's. She asked the good woman what kind of colors looked well with black; not black fabrics, but a black skin.

"I have a little friend to fit out," she said.

"A *black* friend?" said the dressmaker.

"A black friend," said Mrs. Ellsworth.

|||

Some days later Ormond Hunter reported on what his maid knew about Oceola. It seemed that the two belonged to the same church, and although the maid did not know Oceola very well, she knew what everybody said about her in the church. Yes, indeedy! Oceola were a right nice girl, for sure, but it certainly were a shame she were giving all her money to that man what stayed with her and what she was practically putting through college so he could be a doctor.

"Why," gasped Mrs. Ellsworth, "the poor child is being preyed upon."

"It seems to me so," said Ormond Hunter.

"I must get her out of Harlem," said Mrs. Ellsworth, "at once. I believe it's worse than Chinatown."

"She might be in a more artistic atmosphere," agreed Ormond Hunter. "And with her career launched, she probably won't want that man anyhow."

"She won't need him," said Mrs. Ellsworth. "She will have her art."

But Mrs. Ellsworth decided that in order to increase the rapprochement between art and Oceola, something should be done now, at once. She asked the girl to come down to see her the next day, and when it was time to go home, the white woman said, "I have a half-hour before dinner. I'll drive you up. You know I've never been to Harlem."

"All right," said Oceola. "That's nice of you."

But she didn't suggest the white lady's coming in, when they drew up before a rather sad-looking apartment house on 134th Street. Mrs. Ellsworth had to ask could she come in.

"I live on the fifth floor," said Oceola, "and there isn't any elevator."

"It doesn't matter, dear," said the white woman, for she meant to see the inside of this girl's life, elevator or no elevator.

The apartment was just as she thought it would be. After all, she had read Thomas Burke on Limehouse. And here was just one more of those holes in the wall, even if it was five stories high. The windows looked down on slums. There were only four rooms, small as maids' rooms, all of them. An upright piano almost filled the parlor. Oceola slept in the dining-room. The roomer slept in the bed-chamber beyond the kitchen.

"Where is he, darling?"

"He runs on the road all summer," said the girl. "He's in and out."

"But how do you breathe in here?" asked Mrs. Ellsworth. "It's so small. You must have more space for your soul, dear. And for a grand piano. Now, in the Village . . ."

"I do right well here," said Oceola.

"But in the Village where so many nice artists live we can get . . ."

"But I don't want to move yet. I promised my roomer he could stay till fall."

"Why till fall?"

"He's going to Meharry then."

"To marry?"

"Meharry, yes m'am. That's a colored Medicine school in Nashville."

"Colored? Is it good?"

"Well, it's cheap," said Oceola. "After he goes, I don't mind moving."

"But I wanted to see you settled before I go away for the summer."

"When you come back is all right. I can do till then."

"Art is long," reminded Mrs. Ellsworth, "and time is fleeting, my dear."

"Yes, m'am," said Oceola, "but I gets nervous if I start worrying about time."

So Mrs. Ellsworth went off to Bar Harbor for the season, and left the man with Oceola.

IV

That was some years ago. Eventually art and Mrs. Ellsworth triumphed. Oceola moved out of Harlem. She lived in Gay Street west of Washington Square where she met Genevieve Taggard, and Ernestine Evans, and two or three sculptors, and a cat-painter who was also a protegee of Mrs. Ellsworth. She spent her days practicing, playing for friends of her patron, going to concerts, and reading books about music. She no longer had pupils or rehearsed the choir, but she still loved to play for Harlem house parties—for nothing—now that she no longer needed the money, out of sheer love of jazz. This rather disturbed Mrs. Ellsworth, who still believed in art of the old school, portraits that really and truly looked like people, poems about nature, music that had soul in it, not syncopation. And she felt the dignity of art. Was it in keeping with genius, she wondered, for Oceola to have a studio full of white and colored people every Saturday night (some of them actually drinking gin *from bottles*) and dancing to the most tom-tom–like music she had ever heard coming out of a grand piano? She wished she could lift Oceola up bodily and take her away from all that, for art's sake.

So in the spring, Mrs. Ellsworth organized weekends in the up-state mountains where she had a little lodge and where Oceola could look from the high places at the stars, and fill her soul with the vastness of the eternal, and forget about jazz. Mrs. Ellsworth really began to hate jazz—especially on a grand piano.

If there were a lot of guests at the lodge, as there sometimes were, Mrs. Ellsworth might share the bed with Oceola. Then she would read aloud Tennyson or Browning before turning out the light, aware all the time of the electric strength of that brown-black body beside her, and of the deep drowsy voice asking what the poems were about. And then Mrs. Ellsworth would feel very motherly toward this dark girl whom she had taken under her wing on the wonderful road of art, to nurture and love until she became a great interpreter of the piano. At such times the elderly white woman was glad her late husband's money, so well invested, furnished her with a large surplus to devote to the needs of her protegees, especially to Oceola, the blackest—and most interesting of all.

Why the most interesting?

Mrs. Ellsworth didn't know, unless it was that Oceola really was talented, terribly alive, and that she looked like nothing Mrs. Ellsworth had ever been near before. Such a rich velvet black, and such a hard young body! The teacher of the piano raved about her strength.

"She can stand a great career," the teacher said. "She has everything for it."

"Yes," agreed Mrs. Ellsworth, thinking, however, of the Pullman porter at Meharry, "but she must learn to sublimate her soul."

So for two years then, Oceola lived abroad at Mrs. Ellsworth's expense. She studied with Philippe, had the little apartment on the Left Bank, and learned about Debussy's African background. She met many black Algerian and French West Indian students, too, and listened to their interminable arguments ranging from Garvey to Picasso to Spengler to Jean Cocteau, and thought they all must be crazy. Why did they or anybody argue so much about life or art? Oceola merely lived—and loved it. Only the Marxian students seemed sound to her for they, at least, wanted people to have enough to eat. That was important, Oceola thought, remembering, as she did, her own sometimes hungry years. But the rest of the controversies, as far as she could fathom, were based on air.

Oceola hated most artists, too, and the word *art* in French or English. If you wanted to play the piano or paint pictures or write books, go ahead! But why talk so much about it? Montparnasse was worse in that respect than the Village. And as for the cultured Negroes who were always saying art would break down color lines, art could save the race and prevent lynchings! "Bunk!" said Oceola. "My ma and pa were both artists when it came to making music, and the white folks ran them out of town for being dressed up in Alabama. And look at the Jews! Every other artist in the world's a Jew, and still folks hate them."

She thought of Mrs. Ellsworth (dear soul in New York), who never made uncomplimentary remarks about Negroes, but frequently did about Jews. Of little Menuhin she would say, for instance, "He's a *genius*—not a Jew," hating to admit his ancestry.

In Paris, Oceola especially loved the West Indian ball rooms where the black colonials danced the beguine. And she liked the entertainers at Bricktop's. Sometimes late at night there, Oceola would take the piano and beat out a blues for Brick and the assembled guests. In her playing of Negro folk music, Oceola never doctored it up, or filled it full of classical runs, or fancy falsities. In the blues she made the bass notes throb like tom-toms, the trebles cry like little flutes, so deep in the earth and so high in the sky that they understood everything. And when the night-club crowd would get up and dance to her blues, and Bricktop would yell, "Hey! Hey!" Oceola felt as happy as if she were performing a Chopin étude for the nicely gloved Oh's and Ah-ers in a Crillon salon.

Music, to Oceola, demanded movement and expression, dancing and living to go with it. She liked to teach, when she had the choir, the singing of those rhythmical Negro spirituals that possessed the power to pull colored folks out of their seats in the amen corner and make them prance and shout in the aisles for Jesus. She never liked those fashionable colored churches where shouting and movement were discouraged and looked down upon, and where New England hymns instead of spirituals were sung. Oceola's background was too well-grounded in Mobile, and Billy Kersands' Minstrels, and the Sanctified churches where religion was a joy, to stare mystically over the top of a grand piano like white folks and imagine that Beethoven had nothing to do with life, or that Schubert's love songs were only sublimations.

Whenever Mrs. Ellsworth came to Paris, she and Oceola

spent hours listening to symphonies and string quartettes and pianists. Oceola enjoyed concerts, but seldom felt, like her patron, that she was floating on clouds of bliss. Mrs. Ellsworth insisted, however, that Oceola's spirit was too moved for words at such times—therefore she understood why the dear child kept quiet. Mrs. Ellsworth herself was often too moved for words, but never by pieces like Ravel's *Bolero* (which Oceola played on the phonograph as a dance record) or any of the compositions of *les Six*.

What Oceola really enjoyed most with Mrs. Ellsworth was not going to concerts, but going for trips on the little river boats in the Seine; or riding out to old chateaux in her patron's hired Renault; or to Versailles, and listening to the aging white lady talk about the romantic history of France, the wars and uprising, the loves and intrigues of princes and kings and queens, about guillotines and lace handkerchiefs, snuff boxes and daggers. For Mrs. Ellsworth had loved France as a girl, and had made a study of its life and lore. Once she used to sing simple little French songs rather well, too. And she always regretted that her husband never understood the lovely words—or even tried to understand them.

Oceola learned the accompaniments for all the songs Mrs. Ellsworth knew and sometimes they tried them over together. The middle-aged white woman loved to sing when the colored girl played, and she even tried spirituals. Often, when she stayed at the little Paris apartment, Oceola would go into the kitchen and cook something good for late supper, maybe an oyster soup, or fried apples and bacon. And sometimes Oceola had pigs' feet.

"There's nothing quite so good as a pig's foot," said Oceola, "after playing all day."

"Then you must have pigs' feet," agreed Mrs. Ellsworth.

And all this while Oceola's development at the piano blossomed into perfection. Her tone became a singing wonder and her interpretations warm and individual. She gave a concert in Paris, one in Brussels, and another in Berlin. She got the press notices all pianists crave. She had her picture in lots of European papers. And she came home to New York a year after the stock market crashed and nobody had any money—except folks like Mrs. Ellsworth who had so much it would be hard to ever lose it all.

Oceola's one time Pullman porter, now a coming doctor, was graduating from Meharry that spring. Mrs. Ellsworth saw her dark protegee go South to attend his graduation with tears in her eyes. She thought that by now music would be enough, after all those years under the best teachers, but alas, Oceola was not yet sublimated, even by Philippe. She wanted to see Pete.

Oceola returned North to prepare for her New York concert in the fall. She wrote Mrs. Ellsworth at Bar Harbor that her doctor boyfriend was putting in one more summer on the railroad, then in the autumn he would intern at Atlanta. And Oceola said that he had asked her to marry him. Lord, she was happy!

It was a long time before she heard from Mrs. Ellsworth. When the letter came, it was full of long paragraphs about the beautiful music Oceola had within her power to give the world. Instead, she wanted to marry and be burdened with children! Oh, my dear, my dear!

Oceola, when she read it, thought she had done pretty well knowing Pete this long and not having children. But she wrote back that she didn't see why children and music couldn't go together. Anyway, during the present depression, it was pretty hard for a beginning artist like herself to book a concert tour—so she might just as well be married awhile. Pete, on his last run in from St. Louis, had suggested that they have the wedding at Christmas in the South. "And he's impatient, at that. He needs me."

This time Mrs. Ellsworth didn't answer by letter at all. She was back in town in late September. In November, Oceola played at Town Hall. The critics were kind, but they didn't go wild. Mrs. Ellsworth swore it was because of Pete's influence on her protegee.

"But he was in Atlanta," Oceola said.

"His spirit was here," Mrs. Ellsworth insisted. "All the time you were playing on that stage, he was here, the monster! Taking you out of yourself, taking you away from the piano."

"Why, he wasn't," said Oceola. "He was watching an operation in Atlanta."

But from then on, things didn't go well between her and her patron. The white lady grew distinctly cold when she received Oceola in her beautiful drawing room among the jade vases and amber cups worth thousands of dollars. When Oceola would have to wait there for Mrs. Ellsworth, she was afraid to move for fear she might knock something over— that would take ten years of a Harlemite's wages to replace, if broken.

Over the tea cups, the aging Mrs. Ellsworth did not talk any longer about the concert tour she had once thought she might finance for Oceola, if no recognized bureau took it up. Instead, she spoke of that something she believed Oceola's fingers had lost since her return from Europe. And she wondered why any one insisted on living in Harlem.

"I've been away from my own people so long," said the girl, "I want to live right in the middle of them again."

Why, Mrs. Ellsworth wondered further, did Oceola, at her last concert in a Harlem church, not stick to the classical items listed on the program. Why did she insert one of her own variations on the spirituals, a syncopated variation from the Sanctified Church, that made an old colored lady rise up and cry out from her pew, "Glory to God this evenin'! Yes! Hallelujah! Whooo-oo!" right at the concert? Which seemed most undignified to Mrs. Ellsworth, and unworthy of the teachings of Philippe. And furthermore, why was Pete coming up to New York for Thanksgiving? And who had sent him the money to come?

"Me," said Oceola. "He doesn't make anything interning."

"Well," said Mrs. Ellsworth, "I don't think much of him." But Oceola didn't seem to care what Mrs. Ellsworth thought, for she made no defense.

Thanksgiving evening, in bed, together in a Harlem apartment, Pete and Oceola talked about their wedding to come. They would have a big one in a church with lots of music. And Pete would give her a ring. And she would have on a white dress, light and fluffy, not silk. "I hate silk," she said. "I hate expensive things." (She thought of her mother being buried in a cotton dress, for they were all broke when she died. Mother would have been glad about her marriage.) "Pete," Oceola said, hugging him in the dark, "let's live in Atlanta, where there are lots of colored people, like us."

"What about Mrs. Ellsworth?" Pete asked. "She coming down to Atlanta for our wedding?"

"I don't know," said Oceola.

"I hope not, 'cause if she stops at one of them big hotels,

I won't have you going to the back door to see her. That's one thing I hate about the South—where there're white people, you have to go to the back door."

"Maybe she can stay with us," said Oceola. "I wouldn't mind."

"I'll be damned," said Pete. "You want to get lynched?"

But it happened that Mrs. Ellsworth didn't care to attend the wedding, anyway. When she saw how love had triumphed over art, she decided she could no longer influence Oceola's life. The period of Oceola was over. She would send checks, occasionally, if the girl needed them, besides, of course, something beautiful for the wedding, but that would be all. These things she told her the week after Thanksgiving.

"And Oceola, my dear, I've decided to spend the whole winter in Europe. I sail on December eighteenth. Christmas—while you are marrying—I shall be in Paris with my precious Antonio Bas. In January, he has an exhibition of oils in Madrid. And in the spring, a new young poet is coming over whom I want to visit Florence, to really know Florence. A charming white-haired boy from Omaha whose soul has been crushed in the West. I want to try to help him. He, my dear, is one of the few people who live for their art—and nothing else. . . . Ah, such a beautiful life! . . . You will come and play for me once before I sail?"

"Yes, Mrs. Ellsworth," said Oceola, genuinely sorry that the end had come. Why did white folks think you could live on nothing but art? Strange! Too strange! Too strange!

V

The Persian vases in the music room were filled with long-stemmed lilies that night when Oceola Jones came down from Harlem for the last time to play for Mrs. Dora Ellsworth. Mrs. Ellsworth had on a gown of black velvet, and a collar of pearls about her neck. She was very kind and gentle to Oceola, as one would be to a child who has done a great wrong but doesn't know any better. But to the black girl from Harlem, she looked very cold and white, and her grand piano seemed like the biggest and heaviest in the world—as Oceola sat down to play it with the technique for which Mrs. Ellsworth had paid.

As the rich and aging white woman listened to the great roll of Beethoven sonatas and to the sea and moonlight of the Chopin nocturnes, as she watched the swaying dark strong shoulders of Oceola Jones, she began to reproach the girl aloud for running away from art and music, for burying herself in Atlanta and love—love for a man unworthy of lacing up her boot straps, as Mrs. Ellsworth put it.

"You could shake the stars with your music, Oceola. Depression or no depression, I could make you great. And yet you propose to dig a grave for yourself. Art is bigger than love."

"I believe you, Mrs. Ellsworth," said Oceola, not turning away from the piano. "But being married won't keep me from making tours, or being an artist."

"Yes, it will," said Mrs. Ellsworth. "He'll take all the music out of you."

"No, he won't," said Oceola.

"You don't know, child," said Mrs. Ellsworth, "what men are like."

"Yes, I do," said Oceola simply. And her fingers began to wander slowly up and down the keyboard, flowing into the soft and lazy syncopation of a Negro blues, a blues that deepened and grew into rollicking jazz, then into an earth-throbbing rhythm that shook the lilies in the Persian vases of Mrs. Ellsworth's music room. Louder than the voice of the white woman who cried that Oceola was deserting beauty, deserting her real self, deserting her hope in life, the flood of wild syncopation filled the house, then sank into the slow and singing blues with which it had begun.

The girl at the piano heard the white woman saying, "Is this what I spent thousands of dollars to teach you?"

"No," said Oceola simply. "This is mine. . . . Listen! . . . How sad and gay it is. Blue and happy—laughing and crying. . . . How white like you and black like me. . . . How much like a man. . . . And how like a woman. . . . Warm as Pete's mouth. . . . These are the blues. . . . I'm playing."

Mrs. Ellsworth sat very still in her chair looking at the lilies trembling delicately in the priceless Persian vases, while Oceola made the bass notes throb like tom-toms deep in the earth.

O, if I could holler

sang the blues,

> *Like a mountain jack,*
> *I'd go up on de mountain*

sang the blues,

>*And call my baby back.*

"And I," said Mrs. Ellsworth rising from her chair, "would stand looking at the stars."

The Collected Poems of Langston Hughes

Spanning five decades and comprising 868 poems, this magnificent volume is the definitive sampling of a writer who has been called the poet laureate of African America. Here, for the first time, are all the poems that Langston Hughes published during his lifetime. Lyrical and pungent, passionate and polemical, the result is a treasure of a book, the essential collection of a poet whose words have entered our common language.
Poetry/0-679-76408-9

The Panther & the Lash

The last—and the most explicitly political—book of verse by one of the great poets of our century. Hughes's last collection of poems, originally published just before his death in 1967, addresses the racial politics of the 1960s. It includes "Prime," "Motto," "Dream Deferred," "Frederick Douglass: 1817–1895," "Still Here," "Birmingham Sunday," "History," "Slave," "Warning," and "Daybreak in Alabama."
Poetry/0-679-73659-X

Selected Poems of Langston Hughes

The classic collection by the lyric voice of the Harlem Renaissance, whose poetry launched a revolution among black writers in America. Hughes celebrates the experience of men and women who had previously been invisible, in language that merges the spoken with the sung.

Poetry/0-679-72818-X

The Ways of White Folks

In these acrid and poignant stories, Hughes depicts black people colliding—sometimes humorously, more often tragically—with whites in the 1920s and '30s.

Fiction/0-679-72817-1